TEACHINGS OF VIMALAKĪRTI

The Vimalakīrti Nirdeśa contains pieces of doctrinal exposition which touch upon some of the most profound philosophical themes of Buddhism. A short Māhāyana scripture, it is rich with elements of magic, poetry, drama and biography. Setting no limits upon spiritual potential of the individual, it encourages all beings to aspire for the highest conceivable—even the highest inconceivable goal of all spiritual life—supreme perfect Enlightenment.

TEACHINGS OF VIMALAKĪRTI

Demonstration through Magic and Miracles

SANGHARAKSHITA

New Age Books

ISBN: 81-7822-269-8

First Indian Edition: Delhi, 2007

This edition is published by arrangement with Windhorse Publications.

Text illustrations: Varaprabha

Published by
NEW AGE BOOKS
A-44 Naraina, Phase I
New Delhi-110 028 (INDIA)
Email: nab@vsnl.in
Website: www.newagebooksindia.com

For Sale in South Asia Only

Printed in India
at Shri Jainendra Press
A-45 Naraina Phase-I, New Delhi-110 028

Contents

Editor's Preface

It must have been a disturbing and unsettling experience to meet the Buddha in person two-and-a-half thousand years ago in northern India. The examples of such meetings that we find in the Buddhist scriptures give the impression that those who encountered him were often fascinated, awe-struck, and inspired; but occasionally they seem to have been perplexed, nonplussed, even irritated. For some, their existential situation was radically clarified 'as if a lamp were brought into the darkness, so that those with eyes could see what was there'. But others, intrigued though they were, found their meeting with him difficult and his message beyond their grasp. 'Profound is this teaching, hard to see, hard to comprehend, good, excellent, beyond the sphere of reasoning, subtle, to be understood only by the wise.'

If the Buddha's contemporaries sometimes found it hard to relate to him, it is surely even harder for us, so much further away from him in time, space, and culture. Śākyamuni led a very different life-style from most of us: as an 'outsider', a religious mendicant dependent on alms. However, in the Pali scriptures he is still a recognizably human figure. In contrast, the Mahāyāna sūtras present the Buddha as an archetypal figure, living in a splendid and imaginal realm: still fascinating but, apparently at least, still more distant and difficult to comprehend. In the

Vimalakīrti-nirdeśa or 'Teaching of Vimalakīrti' Śākyamuni's remoteness from us is pointed up by the person of Vimalakīrti, introduced to us as a prosperous city-dweller, married with a family, a respected citizen, a popular man-about-town. Here is someone whose life and concerns might seem to resemble our own.

But Vimalakīrti's similarity to his fellow citizens of Vaiśālī – and to many of us – is more apparent than actual. Sangharakshita points out that it would be a serious mistake to regard him as an example of the average layman, either two-and-a-half thousand years ago or now. As the narrative of the *Vimalakīrti-nirdeśa* unfolds, we come to realize that Vimalakīrti, with his depth of spiritual understanding and his ability to demonstrate it through magic and miracles, is almost the Buddha's equal. In other words, he is not what he seems to be.

Why did the Buddhist tradition produce such a figure as Vimalakīrti? What is his function? And why has Sangharakshita, one of the leading interpreters of the Dharma in the modern West, chosen to point him out to us through this series of explorations of themes from the *Vimalakīrti-nirdeśa*?

In a way, it is what Vimalakīrti seems to be that matters. It is because he gets on well with everybody, because he can be 'all things to all men', that he is able to teach the Dharma so effectively and so dramatically, not just in his meetings with the ordinary people of the city, but also in his casual but electrifying confrontations with Arhants and Bodhisattvas. He relates directly, with an uncompromising clarity and compassionate energy that responds to the needs of the immediate situation. He is skilful means personified, skilful means in action, in a manner that, later on in the development of Buddhism, was to flower more fully in the figure of the Tantric guru.

So Vimalakīrti, like the historical Buddha, is a fascinating and unsettling figure. But he too is now far distant from us. For his teachings to affect our lives in the way that they affected those around him, we need those teachings applied to our own situation. We need to understand the significance of who Vimalakīrti was and what he did for who we are and how we behave. The general spiritual or cultural interest which may lead us to pick the *Vimalakīrti-nirdeśa* off the bookshop shelf will not be enough. We will – almost certainly – need help in seeing its relevance to the process of our own spiritual growth. Sangharakshita's guidance, drawing on a lifetime of scholarship and reflection, enables us to enter the exotic world of the Mahāyāna sūtras, and to dwell on the beauty and strangeness of which they speak, allowing their meaning to emerge and unfold for us.

The lectures on which this book is based were given in London sixteen years ago (in 1979). As I heard them then, I remember imagining how followers of the Dharma over the centuries must have listened to their teachers expounding and explaining it anew for their age; I felt that I myself was part of the long tradition of 'hearers' or *śrāvakas*. Preparing Sangharakshita's original spoken words for publication has therefore been a wonderful opportunity to contemplate the richness of his exposition more deeply. This has involved studying the three English translations of the *Vimalakīrti-nirdeśa* and also the transcription of Sangharakshita's seminar on the lectures, held at Padmaloka Retreat Centre in Norfolk in 1987. Some of that material has been incorporated into the present text.

As Sangharakshita remarks, the *Vimalakīrti-nirdeśa* contains many different kinds of writing. As I read through the transcriptions of his lectures, it struck me that they too exhibit a similar range of moods and styles. We move from explanations of Buddhist metaphysics to cultural critique, from personal anecdote to poetry, from humour and irony to direct advice and exhortation to live more creatively and honestly. Major themes from the *Vimalakīrti-nirdeśa* are drawn out and elucidated: how a Buddha-land is actually created; history versus myth; religion as means, not end; and so on. The import of seemingly trivial passing incidents is noticed and commented on: Śāriputra's worry about chairs, for example, discussed at the beginning of Chapter 6. We even find, in Chapter 3, the writers of book-jacket blurbs being given the same incisive sort of treatment as that meted out by Vimalakīrti to the Arhants and Bodhisattvas.

I would like to express my gratitude to all those who have enabled the creation of this book; primarily, of course, to the Venerable Sangharakshita, my teacher. Dharmachakra Tapes made the recordings available, and the original transcriptions were produced by Claire Phillips, Liz Graham, Dharmacari Silabhadra, and Jill Warner. I must also thank Dharmacarini Vidyadevi and Dharmacari Jinananda for their helpful editorial suggestions and additional work on the text, and all at Windhorse Publications who have helped to see the project through. My appreciation also goes to Dharmacarini Varaprabha, who has enhanced the text with her illustrations.

Prajnananda
Spoken Word Project
Bristol
May 1995

1

The Magic of a Mahāyāna Sūtra

Nearly all of us share a particular perception of our own lives which we know to be essentially false. This perception is that our lives tend to be characterized by a certain *sameness*. We spend our time doing much the same sort of things, day after day, even year after year. However much we try to introduce variety, interest, and excitement into our lives, we settle into routines; patterns of one kind or another develop; at the very least we all have to perform all sorts of ordinary human functions – getting dressed, eating, defecating, sleeping – day after day. And we have a sense that our experience of the things we do every day or every week is just the same every time. Of course we know that this is not really the case. We may be washing up the same dishes every day, but we don't wash them in exactly the same circumstances. Each time we wash the dishes is a unique, unrepeatable occasion. Every time we meet a friend – even if we see them every day – it is really for the first time. Every moment of our lives is unique.

Unfortunately, it is all too easy to forget this. We tend to feel that we are doing the same old things in the same old way, day in, day out. Routine and habit seem to drive all the freshness and spontaneity out of life. This can happen not just in our everyday, ordinary lives, but in our spiritual lives as well. Spiritual life is all about change, development, growth. We know that every time we meditate, for instance, it is a completely new experience. We know that it is not even just a question of every time. There is only ever just one time. Each experience, by its very nature, is unrepeatable. This perception of the uniqueness of our experience is what in the Buddhist tradition is known as 'beginner's mind'. But if we are honest we have to admit that we don't always experience this beginner's mind, that our spiritual practice can feel just as flat, dull, and stale as everything else.

If we are beset by this kind of spiritual ennui, it is vital that we shake it off, that we get completely away from any feeling that life – even spiritual life – is dull and boring. From time to time we need to let go of what seems ordinary, safe, comprehensible, and allow ourselves to experience – at least in imagination – some other universe, some other dimension of being, some other system of things. The answer, we may find, is to enter, from time to time, the mysterious world of a Mahāyāna sūtra. We can, if we choose, take a plunge into the unfamiliar, extraordinary – even bizarre – world of a work like the *Vimalakīrti-nirdeśa*, a world where all the familiar landmarks are removed, a world where we may feel that we are being turned completely upside-down.

The *Vimalakīrti-nirdeśa* contains pieces of straightforward doctrinal exposition which touch upon some of the most profound philosophical themes of Buddhism. It also contains passages of lavish description, including descriptions of all sorts of magical feats and happenings. It contains poetry, even poetry in the formal sense of the term. It contains elements of biography and autobiography and reminiscence, and even episodes of high drama – together with quite a bit of humour. Altogether it is an exuberant and complex work, surprisingly so when one considers how short it is. It consists of only fourteen quite brief chapters – the English translation is just about one hundred pages. It is no longer than a long short story, yet it brings together quite a number of very important themes.

Before we take our first step into this rich and strange world, a few words of explanation about the origin of the text are probably in order. It is, to begin with, a Mahāyāna text. The Sanskrit word *Mahāyāna* means simply 'the great way' (*mahā*, 'great', and *yāna*, 'way'). So the Mahāyāna is that form of Buddhism which sets no limit whatever upon the spiritual potential of the individual. It encourages all living beings without exception to aim at the highest conceivable – even the highest inconceivable – goal of the spiritual life: supreme perfect Enlightenment.

One who aims at this supreme perfect Enlightenment not only for their own sake but for the benefit of all beings is known as a Bodhisattva, a being (*sattva*) dedicated to Awakening (*bodhi*). To put it very simply, you could say that for the Mahāyāna the Bodhisattva is the ideal Buddhist. It's what every Buddhist would like to become. And you become a Bodhisattva by developing in yourself those qualities which will give rise to what is called the Bodhicitta: the urge or will to Enlightenment. The path of the Bodhisattva begins when you take the Four Great Vows:

However innumerable beings are, I vow to deliver them;
However inexhaustible the passions are, I vow to extinguish them;
However immeasurable the teachings are, I vow to master them;
However incomparable the Buddha-Truth is, I vow to attain it.

These magnificent, awe-inspiring vows may seem like a tall order, to say the least. What we have to understand here is that there is not really any question of our ordinary limited self taking these vows as though it were making them part of itself. It is more that, in taking the vows, the ordinary self opens itself up to the forces of Wisdom and Compassion which they represent, allowing itself to be inspired and transformed by them, allowing Wisdom and Compassion to work through it. So these Four Great Vows express the essential spirit of the tradition out of which this sūtra emerged.

The word sūtra means simply 'thread', especially in the sense of a connecting thread. In the Buddhist context, sūtras are a particular type or class of Buddhist canonical text, so called because they usually deal with a number of different topics in a more or less connected fashion. So prominent is this class of text within the Buddhist canon that the 'sūtras' have become almost synonymous with what in the West we tend to call the Buddhist scriptures.

However, it is a little misleading to think of these texts as 'scriptures'. The word 'scripture' literally means something written down, but the sūtras were not originally preserved in written form. The Buddha himself, as far as we know, never wrote anything at all. As he travelled around north-eastern India, meeting people and teaching them, he communicated entirely by means of the spoken word. He communicated the Dharma orally, face to face, directly – as much of it as his listeners could assimilate, as much of it as they could bear.

And those who came into contact with him remembered what he had said. Sometimes it made a tremendous impression upon them, sometimes it brought about a turning point in their lives, so how could they forget it? It was burned into their hearts, into their minds, into their very being. And as they put the teachings into practice, they absorbed them, became one with them, learned them by heart. In time the Buddha's followers attracted their own disciples, and taught them in the same way – by word of mouth. Their disciples in turn carried on the oral tradition, and in this way the Buddha's teaching was handed down orally in India for several centuries, until it was eventually committed to writing – not all at once, but bit by bit over several hundred years. It is this oral tradition – in written form – which constitutes Buddhist canonical literature. Some sūtras are still extant in the original Pali or Sanskrit languages in which they were first written down, but others are known to us only through ancient Chinese and Tibetan translations.

Broadly speaking, then, a Mahāyāna sūtra is a canonical text in which the Buddha is represented as teaching, directly or indirectly, the Bodhisattva ideal, the ideal of supreme perfect Enlightenment for the benefit of all living beings. There are hundreds, perhaps thousands, of Mahāyāna sūtras in existence: the *Perfection of Wisdom* sūtras, which include the well-known *Diamond Sūtra* and *Heart Sūtra*, the *White Lotus Sūtra*, the *Sūtra of Golden Light*, and many others.

The *Vimalakīrti-nirdeśa*, although a Mahāyana text, cannot really be counted among these sūtras, inasmuch as it is not quite a sūtra in the usual sense. In Sanskrit it is not actually called a sūtra at all, and in the Chinese translations it is called a *ching*. *Ching* is the usual translation of 'sūtra' in Chinese, but the term originally meant 'classic' in the literary sense. The Sanskrit title of the work is simply *Vimalakīrti-nirdeśa*, which means 'the teaching' – or exposition or instruction – 'of Vimalakīrti'. Vimalakīrti's name means something like 'Stainless Glory', 'Immaculate Fame', or 'Pure Repute', and he is represented as a Buddhist layman living in the northern Indian city of Vaiśālī at the time of the Buddha.

The point is that it is Vimalakīrti who does most of the teaching in this work, not the Buddha (that is, Śākyamuni Buddha) himself. If a sūtra is defined as a discourse by the Buddha, there are clear grounds for not giving this title to the *Vimalakīrti-nirdeśa*. However, Śākyamuni does appear in the text at several points, especially the beginning and the end, he does teach, and he does as it were adopt the work at the end. Perhaps, therefore, there is another reason for dispensing with the term sūtra. Perhaps it is that 'sūtra', like 'scripture', suggests something spiritually authoritative. In fact, of course, it does no such thing: 'spiritually authoritative' is really a contradiction in terms. The Buddhist scriptures – as we call them in English – do not, like the Bible, constitute some infallible revelation from God. They are a record of the life and teaching of a supremely and perfectly Enlightened human being, a human being who was the living embodiment of absolute Wisdom and infinite Compassion. None the less, some people probably do read a sūtra as though it *were* Holy Writ, and feel that they have no choice but to accept whatever the Buddha says in it, whether they like it or not; and such a projection of authority may create in them some resistance to the sūtra's message.

But if a particular text is not actually labelled a sūtra, we can avoid the mistake of regarding it as 'spiritually authoritative'. We can read it, in fact, more or less as we would read any other work of the imagination – a novel, a poem, or a short story. If we can read Buddhist texts as literature rather than dogma, as poetry rather than scientific fact or philosophical truth, we may perhaps be more open to their spiritual message. We may even allow ourselves to be captivated – at least a little – by their atmosphere and their magic. (Conversely – this is just a thought – we might try reading works of imagination as though they were sūtras, and in this way open ourselves to their real spiritual content.)

What I am getting at is that sūtras can be approached as sources of inspiration and enjoyment, not as texts that you have to slog your way through because you happen to be a Buddhist. You may have to put in some additional study and reflection – it may take some time and many readings to understand a sūtra deeply and really appreciate it – but some phrases or images may affect you quite powerfully straight away. It is true that we may well feel more at home with Western literature. Most of it is easier to read because it has been written by unenlightened people like ourselves – with all sorts of little glimmers of insight here and there – and it deals generally with ordinary human predicaments with which we can easily identify. But human frailty is not the only possible subject for literature; it is certainly not always the most inspiring and uplifting one. We can also read literature which takes us away from our ordinary human life and its frailties. And this is what the Mahāyāna sūtras are all about – to take us away from the ordinary, to give us a taste of the magical.

Obviously it is difficult to rise to that level of experience, so it's going to be difficult to read sūtras, just as it is to read some of the great works of Western literature. Any work of literature has an effect commensurate with the effort one makes to understand it. It is really a matter of getting into the habit of stretching oneself a bit. If you have a strong enough desire to understand, you will make the effort. This is why translations like Robert A.F. Thurman's version of the *Vimalakīrti-nirdeśa* are so valuable. If the language is beautiful, you can read and enjoy a text even though you don't fully understand it. It is as though the beauty of the language has its own value. One can read and enjoy the Authorized Version of the Bible, for instance, without believing a word of it. The Authorized Version was gradually shaped out of several earlier translations; no doubt more attractive versions of the Mahāyāna sūtras will emerge in a similar way.

We know that the *Vimalakīrti-nirdeśa* is one of the older Mahāyāna sūtras, but we do not know when it was first written down, because the Indian scribes did not date their work. They were not historically and chronologically minded. With the Chinese, however, it was another matter. When they translated Buddhist texts from Sanskrit into Chinese, they recorded not only the name of the translator, together with that of whoever assisted him and the place where he was working, but also the day of the week and the month and the year when he started, and the precise date when he finished as well. The *Vimalakīrti-nirdeśa* must have been a very popular text in China because in the course of the centuries some seven Chinese translations were made, among them versions by Kumārajīva and Hsüan Tsang, the two greatest translators of Buddhist texts to appear in the entire practically two-thousand-year history of Chinese Buddhism.

Kumārajīva's version is remarkable, as are all his versions of Buddhist texts, especially of Mahāyāna sūtras, for its fidelity to the spirit of the original and its great literary beauty. Hsüan Tsang's version, on the other hand, is impressive in its scholarly accuracy and precision. Kumārajīva's version has always been by far the more popular of the two. One complete Tibetan translation is also extant, as well as fragments of translations in various Central Asian languages. The original Sanskrit text of the *Vimalakīrti-nirdeśa* has unfortunately been lost apart from a few short passages which are quoted in Indian Buddhist writings of a later period, for instance Śāntideva's *Śikṣā Samuccaya* and Kamalaśīla's *Bhāvanakrāma*.

In recent times the *Vimalakīrti-nirdeśa* has been translated into a number of modern languages, both Eastern and Western. There are several versions in English, three of which are at present available. We thus have plenty of material in English for the study of this very important text, one of the most fascinating, readable, and inspiring of all Mahāyāna sūtras.

The three English versions current are by Charles Luk, Etienne Lamotte (his French translation having been rendered into English by Sara Boin), and Robert Thurman. Luk's version, based on Kumārajīva, is perhaps the most traditional of the three, in the strict sense of the term 'traditional'.

Lamotte's, based on the Tibetan version and on Hsüan Tsang, is the most scholarly in the academic sense. Thurman's version, the most recent, based mainly on the Tibetan, comes somewhere in between and I would say above these two. It is both traditional and scholarly in the best sense of these terms, but at the same time scholarship has been subordinated to the needs of spiritual understanding. Thurman has also taken great pains with the literary style. The result is almost a model version of an English translation of a Mahāyāna sūtra: traditional, scholarly, and also very readable – a rare combination of qualities, as you will know only too well if you have ploughed your way through more indigestible English translations of Buddhist texts. Reading Thurman's version of the *Vimalakīrti-nirdeśa* is not only a spiritual experience but also a literary one. It is this translation, for the most part, that I will be using as my source text.

The *Vimalakīrti-nirdeśa* has several alternative titles, the most important of which is *Acintya-vimokṣa*, the 'inconceivable emancipation'. It is in terms of emancipation that the goal of the spiritual life has been envisaged in Buddhism from the most ancient times down to the present day: emancipation from craving, from hatred, from delusion, from all that conditions and confines us, from all that distorts our deepest creativity, from all that prevents us from becoming Enlightened. This experience of spiritual emancipation, of absolute liberation, of total freedom, is what the Buddha's teaching is all about, and what essentially it has always been all about.

Vimokṣa is one of a whole group of similar terms very prominent in early Buddhism. In addition to *vimokṣa* and *mokṣa* (Pali: *vimokkha* and *mokkha*), there are also *vimukti* and *mukti* (Pali: *vimutti* and *mutti*). (The prefix *vi-* acts as an emphatic in Pali and Sanskrit.) They all have the same general sense of emancipation, liberation, or freedom, and they are words which occur over and over again in Pali and Sanskrit texts.

In a well-known passage in the *Udāna*, the 'Verses of Uplift', the Buddha says that just as, wherever you take the water from, the mighty ocean has but one taste, the taste of salt, in the same way his teaching – whether you take the Four Noble Truths, the Noble Eightfold Path, the six *pāramitās*, conditioned co-production, *śūnyatā*, or whatever – has but one taste: the taste of freedom.[1]

According to another well-known formula, there are four stages of spiritual development: morality, or uprightness; concentration and meditation, or higher consciousness; transcendental Wisdom, or Insight into Reality; and emancipation. (Here again the term used is *vimutti*.)

Vimutti is also the penultimate stage of the Spiral Path, the spiritual path described in terms of the twelve positive links. Here freedom arises in dependence upon dispassion, a state of complete spiritual serenity or imperturbability. Dispassion in turn arises in dependence upon disentanglement from worldly concerns, which is itself consequent upon the attainment of 'knowledge and vision of things as they really are'. In terms of the Spiral Path, therefore, freedom is again consequent upon Insight.[2]

Sometimes freedom is spoken of as being twofold. *Cetto-vimukti* is the emancipation of the heart, complete freedom from all subjective, emotional, and psychological biases. *Prajñā-vimukti* is the emancipation that comes from wisdom: freedom from all wrong views, all ignorance, all opinions. This twin freedom, of heart and mind, is the summit of human experience.

Then there is the teaching of the eight *vimokṣas*, the eight emancipations or 'releases'. These represent successively more refined levels of meditative experience, a movement from the realm of the senses, the *kāma-loka*, to the *rūpa-loka*, the realm of form, or the archetypal realm, and eventually the *arūpa-loka*, the 'formless realm'. The eighth of these releases corresponds to Enlightenment itself.[3]

Yet another way of describing emancipation is in terms of the three *vimokṣa-mukhas*, or doors to emancipation (also known as the three *samādhis*). These are three different approaches to the realization of the Unconditioned. According to Buddhist tradition, conditioned, mundane existence has three primary characteristics: that is, it is unsatisfactory, impermanent, and insubstantial. Having developed the profound wisdom which penetrates one of these three characteristics – so that you really *see* the unsatisfactoriness, impermanence, and insubstantiality of things – you attain the corresponding emancipation, which gives you a way in, a doorway, to the Unconditioned.[4]

These are just some of the ways in which the Buddhist tradition has expressed the dimension of spiritual experience which it calls *vimokṣa*. But *acintya* means 'inconceivable' or 'unthinkable'; it also suggests 'inexpressible', even 'ungraspable'. The *acintya-vimokṣa* or 'inconceivable emancipation' is an emancipation which is particular to the Buddhas and irreversible Bodhisattvas, and that is really all we can say about it. Because it is inconceivable, it is also inexpressible.

We can go further than that. We can say that *all* emancipations, to the extent that they are emancipations, are inconceivable. Indeed, emancipation is always emancipation *from* something – the term has no meaning except in relation to a previous state of bondage or imprisonment. And when we have always been in a particular state we cannot really imagine what emancipation from it is like. Indeed, when we have always been in a state of imprisonment, we cannot really get any sense of how imprisoned we are. We may even think that we are not imprisoned at all. We realize the extent to which we were imprisoned only when we have attained release from that imprisonment. If we cannot understand how imprisoned we are, by this and by that, we have little chance of being able to imagine what the state of emancipation from that imprisonment would be like. It is simply inconceivable to us.

We often speak of higher spiritual experience – or even nirvāṇa – as if we knew all about it. But we don't. In fact, we don't really know anything about it at all. We cannot even conceive of it. And it is important to remember this. It means that as we progress in the spiritual life, we are going forward into the unknown. Commitment to the spiritual life is commitment to the unknown. Emancipation, spiritual emancipation, is always emancipation from the known; and the attainment of emancipation is always attainment of the unknown, the unpredictable, the unforeseen, even the unforeseeable. Every emancipation is therefore inconceivable.

But the inconceivable emancipation of the Buddhas and Bodhisattvas is inconceivable – according to the Mahāyāna – in a special and deeper sense. The Mahāyāna, like the Hīnayāna, sees existence not statically, but dynamically; not in terms of entities, but in terms of processes; not in terms of fixed solid unchanging 'things', but in terms of what are called *dharmas* – an untranslatable term which means something like 'phenomena'. According to the Mahāyāna – and this is where it differs from the Hīnayāna – these *dharmas* are in the ultimate sense neither existent nor non-existent. 'Existent' and 'non-existent' are only ideas of our own mind. Because they are neither existent nor non-existent, they naturally neither appear nor disappear. Suffering, for instance, doesn't really appear, and it doesn't really disappear.[5]

Dharmas are thus peaceful from the beginning, and by nature completely – to coin a rather ungainly word – 'nirvanized'. We are accustomed to thinking of nirvāṇa – Enlightenment – as a noun, as representing a state rather than a process, but it does appear in a verbal form in both Pali and Sanskrit. Obviously a verb describes action, and action takes place in time, but 'nirvanization' is not a process taking place in time. It represents the fact that all *dharmas* are in a state of not being affected in reality by either arising or ceasing. But this does not mean that Enlightenment is something static. In short, we really have no words for this state of affairs.

Moreover, because *dharmas* are neither existent nor non-existent, they have no separate characteristics by which they can be distinguished or recognized. Because they have no separate characteristics, they are inconceivable and inexpressible. All *dharmas* are therefore the same – or rather, to avoid giving any impression that Buddhism teaches some sort of monism – not-different. Buddhism does not teach that all the phenomena of existence are reducible to one, whether to one absolute being, like the Brahman of the Vedantic tradition or the 'substance' of Spinoza, or to one matter. Buddhism therefore speaks in terms of 'not-different' or 'not-two' (the Sanskrit is *advaya*) rather than 'the same' or 'one'. We need to avoid any suggestion that the concept of sameness is being reified. Indeed, for the Mahāyāna there can be no question of the reification of any of these terms. Yes, all *dharmas* are 'void of self-nature', as it is expressed; but this voidness is not itself an entity. Voidness is also void.

It is not, I need hardly say, easy to understand this. The inconceivable emancipation really is inconceivable. Not only that. The Bodhisattva sees that existence itself is inconceivable. It is not just that we don't know anything about higher spiritual experiences or nirvāṇa; we don't really know anything about anything at all. It's not that we don't know very much, or that we don't know it very well. This statement is to be taken quite literally: we don't know anything about anything.

But, of course, we think we know, and on that basis we build up all sorts of thought-constructions, all sorts of ideas, attitudes, views, and philosophies. But according to the Mahāyāna these are nothing but delusions. We don't really know anything about anything. And this is something to reflect on from time to time. We are usually so sure that we know what's what. But just take a stone in your hand and feel it, just look at a flower or a tree, and you will see that they are inconceivable. A human being too is inconceivable – staggeringly inconceivable. And, of course, a Buddha, an Enlightened human being, is utterly inconceivable; a Bodhisattva is inconceivable; Buddhism is inconceivable.

So here we have a paradox. The Dharma reveals the nature of existence – but if the nature of existence is inconceivable and not to be fathomed by thought, it cannot be uttered in words. Not only can we not *know* anything about anything; we cannot really *say* anything about anything. If the Buddhas and Bodhisattvas see existence as inconceivable and the Dharma as inexpressible, how is it possible for them to say anything about it? How is the Dharma to be taught?

With this question we begin to get quite close to the strange world of the *Vimalakīrti-nirdeśa*. Even the Buddhas and Bodhisattvas cannot really teach the Dharma in words; instead they demonstrate it through action, and in particular through magical action. According to Buddhist tradition, the Buddhas and Bodhisattvas possess all sorts of magical powers. They can move things from place to place, create things, transform themselves into the likeness of anything they wish. Moreover, they can do all this on a cosmic scale. They can move whole universes, and play with space and time.

In chapter 5 of the *Vimalakīrti-nirdeśa*, for example, Vimalakīrti prepares for the visit of Mañjuśrī (the Bodhisattva of Wisdom) and a great crowd of various beings by magically causing the contents of his house to vanish. When the visitors arrive, nothing is to be seen except Vimalakīrti lying on his bed, apparently ill. In the next chapter he has thirty-two-hundred-thousand thrones transported from a distant Buddha-land so that everyone can sit down, and his house enlarges itself to accommodate them all.

In chapter 10 Vimalakīrti miraculously enables the company to see yet another of the many far-away Buddha-lands. All Buddha-lands have their own particular characteristics; in this one, everything is composed of fragrances, including the food, some of which is brought back by a messenger magically emanated by Vimalakīrti for the purpose. A single vessel of this food proves sufficient to feed everyone present, including the ninety million Bodhisattvas who have accompanied it from whence it came. There is even some left over.

There are many more such happenings throughout the *Vimalakīrti-nirdeśa*. But why on earth does Vimalakīrti do this sort of thing? Why should he make his immediate surroundings invisible and far-distant Buddha-lands visible? Why should he go to the trouble of shifting lion-thrones and magical foodstuffs around? Why bother? All this 'materializing' begins to sound like the stuff of transcendental science fiction.

The simple answer is that in the world of the *Vimalakīrti-nirdeśa*, such magical acts are regarded as being demonstrations of the Dharma. After each magical occurrence the text tells us that many thousands or even hundreds of thousands of beings attain some higher state of spiritual insight, usually 'the spirit of unexcelled, perfect enlightenment' – that is, the Bodhicitta. Their spiritual vision has been broadened and deepened by these magical acts. In chapter 6 Vimalakīrti explicitly states that the ability to perform such acts is an aspect of the inconceivable emancipation. The Bodhisattvas who live in this emancipation, he says, thoroughly realize the relativity of space and time. They can put Mount Sumeru into a mustard seed without shrinking the one or enlarging the other. They can place all living beings in the palm of their hand. They can make a week seem like an age and an age like a week. They have the magical power to transform anyone into anyone and anything into anything.

The *Vimalakīrti-nirdeśa* is not alone among Mahāyāna texts in its attribution of a philosophical significance to magic. In the Mahāyāna, existence itself is frequently compared to a magic show.[6] But how does this square with the Buddha's well-known admonition to his disciples that they should positively refrain from performing miracles?[7] How can magical acts be regarded as demonstrations of the Dharma?

Magic was very popular in India in ancient times, as I believe it still is today. It seems that the Indians have always been rather good at it. Imagine, for example, a wandering magician walking into a village in ancient India one morning. (Perhaps he has left his magic carpet round the corner.) As he arrives, a drum starts to beat, and people begin to gather round, eager and expectant, waiting for something to happen. It's natural to be curious about such things. If a magician came down the street at this very minute, you would probably drop the book and go out to have a look – and rightly so, because you can read a book any old time, but you don't see a magical display every day of the week. In the ancient Indian village, the magician would no doubt start off by doing something quite routine, quite ordinary, the kind of thing that magicians are expected to do. He conjures up, let's say, an elephant. He repeats a certain mantra and instantly, in front of everybody, an elephant appears. There it calmly stands, as large as life: bulky body, flapping ears, waving trunk. People can see it, hear it, perhaps smell it, perhaps even touch it – or think that they can touch it. Maybe some people in the audience even get frightened and run away.

In the modern West we would probably call this a collective hallucination. But the Mahāyāna would point out that the elephant perceived by all those villagers is neither absolutely unreal nor absolutely non-existent. After all, you cannot easily deny the testimony of your own eyes. Everybody in the village knows perfectly well what an elephant looks like – and they have all seen one standing in front of them. Furthermore, it has had an effect, because some people have run away. But at the same time it is not absolutely real, not absolutely existent. The magician made it appear, and sooner or later he will make it disappear.

According to the Mahāyāna, ordinary existence as we experience it is just like this. The *dharmas* are just like this. They are neither existent nor non-existent – not in absolute terms – so they cannot be said really to appear or really to disappear. They are just like the magical illusion. Existence is just like a great collective hallucination. The Mahāyāna also compares it to a dream, an echo, a mirage, a reflection, a ball of foam, and so on. The point of all these comparisons is not that something which is not really there is perceived to exist, but rather that what is perceived to exist is not absolutely existent. Phenomenal existence arises in dependence on causes and conditions, so it is neither absolutely real nor absolutely unreal. 'Absolutely real' here means that which does not arise in dependence on causes and conditions. In terms of the older Buddhist texts, it is what is usually translated as 'the Unconditioned' – the *asaṁskṛta*, literally 'the incomposite', that which is not put together.

But even if everything is in a sense like a magical illusion, we still have to engage with it, because we consider it to be real. When the magician conjures up the elephant, people perceive it and even become frightened enough to run away. Their fright is a real experience – at least relatively real – and something has to be done about it. So the fact that your relative experience is, in a sense, illusory, doesn't mean that you ignore it. You experience it as real, just as the people who perceive the illusory elephant perceive it as real. They don't know that it is illusory. They don't know that their perception has arisen in dependence on the complex of causes and conditions (represented by the magician). Only when they see that there is no elephant there, absolutely existent in its own right, but only a phenomenon that has arisen in dependence on the volition of the magician, can they cease to act as though the elephant were real.

Continuing the traditional Buddhist line of thought, if you were Enlightened, you would perceive the elephant, but you would know that what you were perceiving was a magical illusion, so you would not react to it as you would if you were not Enlightened. Even if it charged towards you, you would know that nothing was going to happen, that it was only an illusion, so you would not try to get out of the way, or experience any fear.

But, to take this illustration a little further, if you were Enlightened and you saw a real elephant charging towards you, you would get out of the way, because you would know that your physical body was on the same level of existence as the elephant's. Even though both are illusory in the metaphysical sense, both are physical bodies. They exist within and belong to the same order of reality, and within that order of reality they can affect each other. But you would still not experience fear, because your mind would be attuned not to relative reality but to Absolute Reality.

In a sense, whether you are Enlightened or not, you see the same object, but you interpret it differently. For instance, things are impermanent, and it is obviously inappropriate to be attached to things which are impermanent. None the less, we do become attached; despite the fact that we 'know' that something is impermanent, we treat it as though it is permanent. And if you see or experience an illusion as an absolute reality and treat it accordingly, that gives rise to unskilful mental states. But if you were Enlightened, you would be fully aware of its impermanence, and would treat it as such.

Using the terms 'illusion' or 'illusory' when discussing Buddhism can create a lot of misunderstanding. The illustration of the magically-produced elephant is an illusion only when it is considered metaphysically, not in terms of ordinary human experience. There is an objective difference between an elephant which is actually an elephant and an elephant which is only an illusory elephant. This is where Mahāyāna Buddhism differs from the Hinduism of the Advaita Vedānta. Vedāntins would use the same illustration to try to show that the elephant conjured up by the magician doesn't exist in reality *at all*. For the Advaita Vedānta, the whole of phenomenal existence is like that; only Ultimate Reality exists.

Some Vedāntins might regard this as an unfair presentation of Śankara's teaching, but many Indian philosophers, including Sri Aurobindo, have taken it to be his actual view – a view which Buddhism would regard as being one-sided. We can see the difference in the positions of the two religions if we consider their usage of the term *māyā*, illusion. In the Advaita Vedānta, *māyā* indicates that which doesn't have any existence at all, but is pure illusion. But in Buddhism it indicates that which has a relative but not an absolute existence. And, of course, Buddhism goes further and says that, in the last analysis, there is no distinction between the relative and the absolute. It is not that the relative is merged into the absolute in a one-sided manner, as in the Advaita Vedānta; both 'relative' and 'absolute' are equally applicable and equally inapplicable to ultimate reality.[8]

So the Mahāyāna does not doubt or question our experience. It is not trying to tell us that nothing exists at all. What it questions is the ultimate validity of the conceptual constructions which we superimpose upon it. Where we go wrong is in interpreting our experience in terms of fixed, solid, unchanging things. This is why the *Vimalakīrti-nirdeśa*, and the Mahāyāna in general, regard magical acts as being demonstrations of the Dharma: because these acts are themselves an illustration of what existence is really like.

It is this magical atmosphere in which the events of the *Vimalakīrti-nirdeśa* unfold. One could spend a lifetime exploring the text and contemplating the vision it presents, but here we will be looking at just a few of its themes. To get an idea of the context in which these themes appear, however, we will begin with a brief survey of the whole work.

Although, as we have seen, the text is not strictly speaking a sūtra, it opens in typical Mahāyāna sūtra fashion, with the Buddha, surrounded by a great assembly of disciples, giving a teaching. On this occasion he is staying in Āmrapālī's Park, on the outskirts of the city of Vaiśālī – Vaiśālī being where the historical Buddha gave a great many of his teachings. And the great assembly surrounding him is made up of all sorts of beings: Arhants, Bodhisattvas, as well as Brahmās, and various non-human beings – gods and deities of all kinds – besides monks and nuns, laymen and laywomen.

Just as the Buddha is about to start teaching, the Bodhisattva Ratnākara arrives from Vaiśālī to visit him, accompanied by no fewer than five hundred Licchavi youths – that is, young men of the tribe whose capital was Vaiśālī – and each of these youths carries with him an umbrella or parasol. These are not to shield them from sun or rain: in ancient India parasols were not just utilitarian, but symbolized sovereignty, or even spiritual sovereignty. And like so many things in Mahāyāna sūtras, these parasols are made of the seven precious substances – gold, pearl, and so on. The Licchavi youths offer these five hundred parasols to the Buddha, and with his magical power he transforms them all into a single enormous precious canopy which covers the entire billion-world galaxy. In this precious canopy every single world and every single being within the galaxy is reflected. After praising the Buddha in a very beautiful hymn, Ratnākara asks him to explain how a Bodhisattva creates and purifies a Buddha-land. We will be going into the Buddha's reply in our Chapter 2, 'Building the Buddha-land'.

In the second chapter of the text, the scene shifts to the city of Vaiśālī and we meet Vimalakīrti himself. He is a great Bodhisattva, even a Buddha, but he lives just like an ordinary layman. He lives at home, seems to have a family, seems to have a job, seems to be like other people. But all this is simply his 'skilful means'. He outwardly adapts himself to people so that he can approach them and teach them the Dharma. And as part of his skilful means, he falls sick – or appears to fall sick. As a result, all sorts of people come to visit him, and he takes the opportunity of teaching them the Dharma. This will be the subject of our Chapter 3, 'On Being "All Things to All Men"'.

In chapters 3 and 4 of the text, we move back to Āmrapālī's Park, where the Buddha airs the suggestion that someone should call on Vimalakīrti and ask him how he is. He asks first the Arhants, beginning with Śāriputra, and then the Bodhisattvas, beginning with Maitreya. But they are all strangely reluctant to meet Vimalakīrti. They have, it seems, encountered him before, and, Arhants or Bodhisattvas though they are, he has treated them all to a very rough time: that is to say, he has ruthlessly exposed the inadequacies of their approach to the Dharma. We will be going into this in our Chapter 4, 'The Transcendental Critique of Religion'.

In the next chapter of the *Vimalakīrti-nirdeśa,* someone finally agrees to visit Vimalakīrti. Mañjuśrī, the Bodhisattva of Wisdom, says he will go, and together with many of those in the assembly he sets out for Vaiśālī. When he arrives at Vimalakīrti's house, he immediately enters into a vigorous dialogue with Vimalakīrti on the nature of emptiness and liberation. Each tries to give the other a real dialectical hammering, but they are very evenly matched.

Once this little transcendental sparring match is over, Mañjuśrī comes to the point and asks Vimalakīrti why he is sick. Vimalakīrti's reply to this question has become very famous. He says that he is sick because beings are sick; his sickness has arisen from great Compassion. He also explains at some length how a 'sick' Bodhisattva should control his mind. Here and in later chapters, we find Mañjuśrī, a mythical figure, and Vimalakīrti, a historical personality, juxtaposed: myth and history face to face. This will be our theme in Chapter 5, 'History Versus Myth in Humanity's Quest For Meaning'.

Chapter 6 of the text deals, as we have seen, with the inconceivable emancipation itself. By his magical power, Vimalakīrti transports thirty-two-hundred-thousand thrones from the Buddha-land of the Buddha Merupradīparāja, which is innumerable Buddha-lands away in the eastern direction. All these thrones, which are apparently miles and miles high, are quite comfortably accommodated in Vimalakīrti's house – a magical feat which demonstrates the relativity of space. Space is only a concept, just as time is only a concept. Vimalakīrti then describes various other magical feats which the Bodhisattva who lives in the inconceivable emancipation is capable of performing.

In chapter 7 Vimalakīrti explains in response to a question from Mañjuśrī how a Bodhisattva should regard all beings. At this point, a goddess who lives in Vimalakīrti's house showers the whole assembly with heavenly flowers. The flowers which land on the Bodhisattvas touch them and fall to the ground, but those which land on the Arhants stick to them. Śāriputra tries, unsuccessfully, to brush them off; monks are not supposed to wear flowers. A dialogue ensues between Śāriputra and the goddess in which she demonstrates her deep understanding of the Dharma and explains the wonderful characteristics of Vimalakīrti's house.

In chapter 8 Vimalakīrti explains how to attain the qualities of a Buddha. For his part, Mañjuśrī then explains what the true family of the Buddha consists in. They both speak in highly paradoxical terms. After this, one of the Bodhisattvas present enquires after Vimalakīrti's family. In India people always want to know all the personal details: who your father is, who your mother is, where they live, whether you are married, how many children you have, and so on, and so on. Vimalakīrti's reply to this questioning is in the form of a series of beautiful verses – indeed, one of the most beautiful passages in the whole work. He says that the Bodhisattva's mother is the Perfection of Wisdom. The Perfection of Wisdom gives birth to him, nurtures and nourishes him. His father is Skilful Means. His wife is Delight in the Dharma. His daughters are Love and Compassion, and his sons are Righteousness and Truth. As for his home, that is meditation on the meaning of the void. Vimalakīrti continues in this way for forty or fifty verses.

Chapter 9 deals with the question of non-duality. Vimalakīrti asks all the Bodhisattvas present to explain their ideas about non-duality, which, in turn, they do. They then ask Mañjuśrī what his explanation of non-duality is. They have all spoken well, he says, but their explanations fall short in that they are all dualistic, whereas non-duality cannot be expressed at all. This statement of Mañjuśrī's is very profound, but he does not get the last word … or rather he does. When he has spoken, he asks Vimalakīrti for his own explanation of non-duality – whereupon Vimalakīrti remains completely silent. This is the famous 'thunder-like silence' of Vimalakīrti. When we come to this incident in our sixth chapter, 'The Way of Non-duality', however, we will find at least something to say.

In chapter 10 of the text we come relatively down to earth. Śāriputra starts worrying about when everybody will be having lunch. After all, monks are not supposed to eat after twelve o'clock. (If you have never been a monk, you won't know how important this is.) Vimalakīrti knows what Śāriputra is thinking; he has that magical power too. And it is here that he conjures up a beautiful young Bodhisattva, golden in colour, whom he sends off to a Buddha-land called 'Fragrant with all Fragrances' to get some food. This Bodhisattva returns with a bowl containing fragrant ambrosia, and with him come ninety million other Bodhisattvas who all somehow manage to squeeze into Vimalakīrti's house. The ambrosia, strange to say, provides more than enough to feed the whole assembly. In response to a question from Vimalakīrti, the Bodhisattvas who have just arrived say that the Buddha of their Buddha-land does not teach the Dharma by means of sound and language. He teaches it by means of perfumes. This will be the subject of our seventh chapter, 'The Mystery of Human Communication'.

In chapter 11 of the text we return to Āmrapālī's Park, where the Buddha is teaching all those disciples who did not accompany Mañjuśrī on his visit to Vimalakīrti. While he is teaching, the whole park suddenly gets larger, and everything in it is tinged with a beautiful golden hue. We get the feeling that something is about to happen – and it does. No sooner has the Buddha told Ānanda that Vimalakīrti and Mañjuśrī are coming from Vaiśālī with their retinue than they all arrive. The Buddha proceeds to give a teaching, explaining that different Buddhas teach the Dharma in different ways, yet their Enlightenment and their spiritual realizations are all the same. He also speaks at length on the Emancipation called 'the Destructible and the Indestructible'.

In chapter 12, after Vimalakīrti has explained his perception of the Buddha, Śāriputra wants to know where Vimalakīrti comes from. He is told that the great Bodhisattva comes from Abhirati – 'Great Delight' – the Buddha-land of the Buddha Akṣobhya in the eastern direction. The next thing is that everyone wants to see this marvellous land, so the Buddha asks Vimalakīrti to show it to them and, magically, Vimalakīrti does so.

In chapter 13 Indra, the king of the gods, praises the teaching of the inconceivable emancipation and promises to protect the Dharma. The Buddha then relates how he himself practised the Dharma in a previous existence, following teachings he received from the Buddha of those days, Bhaiṣajyarāja. Among these is the teaching of the four reliances: that one should rely on the meaning of the Dharma, not on the literal expression; on Wisdom, not on ordinary consciousness; on ultimate teachings, not on provisional teachings; and on principles, not on personalities. We will be going into these four reliances in our eighth chapter, 'The Criteria for the Spiritual Life'.

In chapter 14 of the text the Buddha entrusts this teaching of supreme Enlightenment to Maitreya, the future Buddha. Maitreya promises to protect and promote the Dharma, especially the present exposition, which he will ensure is widely taught, copied, talked about, remembered, and understood. All the Bodhisattvas promise likewise, and so do the Four Great Kings, the guardians of the four quarters of the universe. Ānanda, who thinks of everything, asks by what name this exposition of the Dharma is to be known. The Buddha tells him that it is to be called the *Vimalakīrti-nirdeśa*, and amid general happiness and rejoicing, the text closes.

2

BUILDING THE BUDDHA-LAND

ACCORDING TO ANCIENT BUDDHIST COSMOLOGY, space is infinite. And this infinite space is occupied by an infinite number of world systems, each existing on three planes: a plane of sensuous desire, a plane of pure form, and a formless plane. A thousand such world systems make up one small universe; a thousand small universes make up one middling universe; and a thousand middling universes make up one great universe. We could go on, but this should be enough to establish an overall cosmological scale of things.[9]

If the beings living in a great universe are fortunate, they may – whether they know it or not – also be living in a Buddha-land. A Buddha-land is the sphere of spiritual influence of one particular Buddha, one supremely, perfectly Enlightened being who is responsible for the spiritual welfare of all the living beings in all the world systems within that great universe, or even within several great universes. So not only do we have an infinity of world systems; we have also this idea of an infinity of Buddhas – or at least, if that sounds too outrageous, a plurality, a very considerable plurality, of Buddhas.

Not all great universes are fortunate enough to have a Buddha responsible for them. A Buddha is not some sort of god. He starts off as an ordinary human being, just like anybody else. What makes him extraordinary is his commitment to the spiritual life. He takes the Bodhisattva vow, and follows the Bodhisattva path for thousands upon thousands of lives, pursuing his spiritual career within the world systems of the particular great universe for which he will one day have spiritual responsibility. In the course of his Bodhisattva career he comes into contact with an enormous number of living beings, whom he helps to the best of his ability. And eventually, after many, many lives of spiritual endeavour as a Bodhisattva, he becomes, in his last lifetime, a Buddha.

The Mahāyāna tradition draws a distinction between a Buddha's sphere of knowledge, which is conterminous with the whole of conditioned existence, and his sphere of influence, his Buddha-land, which is held to be limited to one or more great universes. A Buddha's knowledge is unlimited because it is an inner realization, not dependent on or manifested through any particular form, however subtle or refined. But his influence on other beings who are by definition not on the same level has to be exerted through a particular form, a particular medium – and that medium is limited. A human historical Buddha – a *nirmāṇakāya* Buddha in the language of the Mahāyāna – has a physical body and physical senses, and his influence is communicated through those. The fact that he is embodied in that way limits his influence.

It is not always clear, however, whether the Buddha whose influence extends over so many worlds in the Mahāyāna sūtras is a *nirmāṇakāya* Buddha (a historical Buddha) or a *sambhogakāya* Buddha (an archetypal Buddha), or a Buddha somewhere between the two. What *is* clear is that a Buddha whose influence extends over many, many worlds is not as limited in his influence as a *nirmāṇakāya* Buddha in the narrowest sense – that is, a human historical Buddha. But however far the Buddha's influence extends, it has a limit, because it proceeds from a Buddha who is limited – limited, that is, with regard to his outward form, whether that outward form belongs to a lower or a higher level. It is only the *dharmakāya* which is unlimited, and it is therefore only on the level of the *dharmakāya* that a Buddha's knowledge has no limit. When the Buddha wants to communicate, when he wants to influence beings, he has to come down a step or two, in order to communicate through his human or archetypal personality with the beings on those lower levels. It is usually said that the *sambhogakāya* is that aspect of the Buddha which communicates with the Bodhisattvas, but it is sometimes said that the *sambhogakāya* has two levels: on one level the Buddha communicates with advanced Bodhisattvas, and on the other he communicates with other Buddhas. If you think in terms of other Buddhas, there is division, there is limitation; but if all those divisions and limitations are removed there is only the *dharmakāya*.[10] On that level there is no question of communication, there is no question of influencing. There is only a non-dual knowledge or intuition. Because in respect of his supreme, perfect Enlightenment one Buddha does not differ from another, in a sense all Buddha-lands are one Buddha-land.

The Mahāyāna does, however, distinguish between two kinds of Buddha-land: pure and impure. An impure Buddha-land is one in which all six realms of sentient existence are found: the realms of the gods, human beings, *āsuras* or anti-gods, hungry ghosts, tormented beings, and animals. In an impure Buddha-land the basic necessities of life – food, clothing, and shelter – are hard to obtain. It is difficult to hear the Dharma, and difficult to come into contact with Buddhas and Bodhisattvas. In short, it is a place where conditions are not at all conducive to spiritual development, where it is difficult for living beings to evolve towards Enlightenment. Our own Buddha-land, in which our Buddha gained Enlightenment, is – and no doubt this will come as no surprise – an impure Buddha-land. It is described in the Mahāyāna sūtras as a dirty, disagreeable, dangerous place, and Bodhisattvas belonging to other Buddha-lands are warned to be very careful when passing through it.

A pure Buddha-land is, of course, the exact opposite. Apart from Buddhas and Bodhisattvas, it contains only gods and human beings. Food, clothing, and shelter appear spontaneously, without anyone having to work to produce them. The sound of the Dharma is everywhere, and everywhere you can come into contact with Buddhas and Bodhisattvas. Conditions are perfectly conducive to spiritual development. The best-known example of a pure Buddha-land is Sukhāvatī, the 'Happy Land' or 'Land of Bliss', which is the Buddha-land of Amitābha, the Buddha of Infinite Light. There are lengthy descriptions of its great beauty in the three 'Pure Land' sūtras, which describe it entirely in terms of flashing jewels, brilliant lights, lotus flowers, music, and perfume. In the midst of Sukhāvatī the Buddha Amitābha, golden in colour (he is elsewhere depicted as a red figure), sits on a magnificent lotus-throne, flanked by his two chief Bodhisattvas, Avalokiteśvara and Mahāsthāmaprāpta. Beings appear in Sukhāvatī, as they do in other Pure Lands, by way of apparitional birth or spontaneous appearance, not as a result of sexual union. And having appeared, they have nothing to do but enjoy being in the presence of Amitābha and his Bodhisattvas, listen to his teaching, and develop spiritually in accordance with it.[11]

The distinction between pure and impure Buddha-lands is not, however, absolute. It is possible for a Buddha to transform an impure Buddha-land into a pure Buddha-land, and vice versa. Purifying a Buddha-land is, in fact, equivalent to building one. Of course, one might well ask why a Buddha should want to transform a pure Buddha-land into an impure one. One answer is that, as we shall see when we come to look at the first chapter of the *Vimalakīrti-nirdeśa,* people find it very difficult to live in a pure Buddha-land. Alternatively, it might be that a pure Buddha-land would be less helpful spiritually to people who need to mature than an impure one. The Buddha might 'create' an impure Buddha-land because that suits certain people better.

Both the question and the answers are based on the assumption that a Buddha literally creates a Buddha-land, whether pure or impure – which we shall find is not the whole truth. But if one thinks in terms of the Buddha transforming a pure Buddha-land into an impure one, it can be only as a skilful means for the sake of those beings who are not able to benefit for one reason or another from a perfectly pure Buddha-land. At the same time – and again, this is a point which will receive dramatic demonstration in the opening chapter of our text – it is said that in the ultimate sense all Buddha-lands are pure. The Buddhas see them as pure even if ordinary beings do not. It is also possible for a Bodhisattva to create a pure Buddha-land in the midst of an impure Buddha-land. Vimalakīrti's house as described in chapter 7 of the *Vimalakīrti-nirdeśa* is a pure Buddha-land of this sort.

A Buddha-land is also known as a 'Buddha-field' (*buddha-kṣetra* in Sanskrit). A field is, of course, something in which seeds are planted and grow, so the suggestion is that living beings, the inhabitants of the *kṣetra,* are like plants to be cultivated, and that the Buddha is, so to speak, a great cosmic gardener. Indeed, the Mahāyāna texts repeatedly describe the Buddhas and Bodhisattvas as 'maturing' or 'ripening' living beings – assisting them gradually, step by step, to spiritual perfection.

This sort of imagery is found very early in the history of Buddhism. Shortly after his Enlightenment, 'our' Buddha, Śākyamuni, had a vision of all living beings as being just like lotus flowers at various stages of development: some sunk deep in the mud, others just beginning to rise up from it; some just buds, others half-open blossoms, and still others almost completely open.[12] Similarly in the *White Lotus Sūtra* the Buddha is compared to the sun, shining down on all beings alike, and his Dharma or Teaching to the rain. Living beings are of course like the trees, shrubs, and other plants, and when the rain falls and the sun shines, they all grow and flourish in their own way.[13] The idea of the Buddha-land or Buddha-field uses the same kind of horticultural imagery.

The building and purifying of the Buddha-land is the main theme of the first chapter of the *Vimalakīrti-nirdeśa*. The chapter begins, as we have seen, in Āmrapālī's garden, the park which Āmrapālī, the erstwhile courtesan, donated, towards the end of her life, to the Buddha and his disciples. The text tells us that the Buddha was staying there with a great gathering of his disciples. There were eight thousand monks – all in their yellow robes, shaven-headed, and presumably with their begging-bowls ready. All of them were Arhants, that is, they had gained Enlightenment on their own individual account. In traditional Buddhist art the Arhant is usually represented as a wrinkled old man bowed down with age, sometimes with a staff. In addition, there were thirty-two thousand Bodhisattvas, who are, by contrast, traditionally depicted as beautiful young princes, sixteen years of age. More than fifty of these Bodhisattvas – including Mañjuśrī and Maitreya – are mentioned by name.

There were also many thousands of gods ('Brahmās, Śakras, Lokapālas, devas') and what we would regard as mythological beings and beasts of different kinds ('nāgas, yakṣas, gandharvas, āsuras, garuḍas, kiṁnaras, and mahoragas') as well as ordinary monks, nuns, laymen, and laywomen. So, we are told, 'surrounded and venerated by these multitudes of many hundreds of thousands of living beings', and towering over them 'just as Sumeru, the king of mountains, looms high over the oceans', the Buddha 'shone, radiated, and glittered as he sat upon his magnificent lion-throne'.[14] So this is the marvellous, extraordinary setting for the whole work – the Buddha preparing to teach the Dharma in the midst of this fantastic assembly.

But before he can get started, he is interrupted by the arrival of the Bodhisattva Ratnākara coming from Vaiśālī, just a little way distant. He is accompanied by no fewer than five hundred Licchavi youths – the Licchavis being the tribe of people whose capital was Vaiśālī – each carrying a parasol made of the seven precious substances. In Mahāyāna sūtras things are often made of these seven precious substances, usually enumerated as gold, silver, pearl, sapphire, ruby, emerald, and diamond (the list varies slightly in different texts).

As soon as they arrive, the youths salute the Buddha, and then, carrying their five hundred precious parasols, they walk round him seven times, keeping him all the time on their right – an ancient Indian way of showing respect often mentioned in the Buddhist texts. Having circumambulated the Buddha in this way, they offer their parasols to him, and by his magical power he proceeds to transform those five hundred parasols into a single precious canopy so enormous that it covers the entire billion-world galaxy. We are told that the contents of the billion-world galaxy are reflected in the interior of this canopy, so that all those present can look up into it and see limitless suns, moons, and stars, limitless heavenly realms, limitless Mount Sumerus, limitless oceans and rivers, limitless villages and cities, limitless people – and limitless Buddhas teaching the Dharma. The voices of all these Buddhas teaching can be distinctly heard echoing in the interior of the canopy. Naturally, the assembly is astonished and delighted at this extraordinary vision, and they all bow down before the Buddha.

Without suggesting that there is some allegorical, point-by-point interpretation of this sequence of events to be attempted, we can perhaps lay down a few pointers as to their significance. The five hundred parasols borne aloft, so brilliant and so colourful, surely represent the spiritual aspirations of those five hundred Licchavi youths – in particular their urge or will towards supreme perfect Enlightenment for the benefit of all beings. In other words, the parasols represent the arisen Bodhicitta.

There are five hundred youths, and therefore five hundred parasols; so you might imagine that there would be five hundred Bodhicittas. But the fact that the parasols are all offered to the Buddha shows us that the spiritual aspirations of the youths all have one and the same object: supreme perfect Enlightenment, as represented by the Buddha himself as he sits there. This shared aspiration acts as a unifying force. It means that their aspirations tend to converge, even to unite, to become one single aspiration. This is why the Buddha transforms the parasols into a single canopy.

But what is that one single aspiration? What does the great canopy represent? As long as we don't take the expression too literally, as long as we take it poetically rather than dogmatically, we can think of it as representing what may be called the 'Cosmic Bodhicitta'. And just as the entire billion-world galaxy is reflected in the canopy, the Cosmic Bodhicitta is aware of, and responsive to, the needs of all sentient beings. It is not collective; at the same time it is not individual in the ordinary sense. It belongs to a mysterious category for which we have as yet no word, a category which also includes the expression 'spiritual community'. This is the possible significance of this incident at a very high level, but we can also explain it in more ordinary terms. It could signify that to the extent that our spiritual aspirations have a common object, they will be united;

and to the extent that they are united, they will be a force for good in the world.

After the offering of the parasols, the Bodhisattva Ratnākara praises the Buddha in a series of beautiful verses: a *stuti*, or 'praising', or what we might call in English a 'hymn'. It is intensely joyful and devotional, full of admiration and reverence for the Buddha; but at the same time – and this is one of the extraordinary features of these Mahāyāna hymns, in fact of the Mahāyāna generally – it is profoundly philosophical in content. It starts like this:

Pure are your eyes, broad and beautiful,
like the petals of a blue lotus.
Pure is your thought, having discovered
the supreme transcendence of all trances.
Immeasurable is the ocean of your virtues,
the accumulation of your good deeds.
You affirm the path of peace.
O Great Ascetic, obeisance to you![15]

Then later we come to a verse which summarizes the philosophical paradox at the heart of the sūtra. Ratnākara says:

All these things arise dependently, from causes,
Yet they are neither existent nor nonexistent.
Therein is neither ego, nor experiencer, nor doer,
Yet no action, good or evil, loses its effects.
Such is your teaching.[16]

At the conclusion of this hymn, Ratnākara asks the Buddha a question on behalf of the five hundred Licchavi youths who have accompanied him. Having taken the Bodhisattva vow, they want the Buddha to explain to them the purification of the Buddha-field of the Bodhisattvas. In other words, Ratnākara wants to know, and they want to know, how to set about building a Buddha-land.

The Buddha is quite pleased with this question, and he answers at some length. He says, to begin with:

'Noble sons, a buddha-field of bodhisattvas is a field of living beings. Why so? A bodhisattva embraces a buddha-field to the same extent that he causes the development of living beings. He embraces a buddha-field to the same extent that living beings become disciplined. He embraces a buddha-field to the same extent that, through entrance into a buddha-field, living beings are introduced to

> the buddha-gnosis. He embraces a buddha-field to the same extent that, through entrance into that buddha-field, living beings increase their holy spiritual faculties. Why so? Noble son, a buddha-field of bodhisattvas springs from the aims of living beings.
>
> 'For example, Ratnākara, should one wish to build in empty space, one might go ahead in spite of the fact that it is not possible to build or to adorn anything in empty space. In just the same way, should a bodhisattva, who knows full well that all things are like empty space, wish to build a buddha-field in order to develop living beings, he might go ahead, in spite of the fact that it is not possible to build or to adorn a buddha-field in empty space.'[17]

He goes on to say that a Bodhisattva's Buddha-field is a field of positive thought, a field of high resolve, a field of virtuous application, a field of the six perfections, a field of the four immeasurables, a field of the thirty-seven aids to Enlightenment, a field of the ten precepts, and so on. And he concludes by saying of a Bodhisattva:

> 'His virtuous application is tantamount to his high resolve, his high resolve is tantamount to his determination, his determination is tantamount to his practice, his practice is tantamount to his total dedication, his total dedication is tantamount to his liberative technique, his liberative technique is tantamount to his development of living beings, and his development of living beings is tantamount to the purity of his buddha-field.
>
> 'The purity of his buddha-field reflects the purity of living beings; the purity of the living beings reflects the purity of his gnosis; the purity of his gnosis reflects the purity of his doctrine; the purity of his doctrine reflects the purity of his transcendental practice; and the purity of his transcendental practice reflects the purity of his own mind.'[18]

At this point Śāriputra, one of the Buddha's chief disciples, who is present in the assembly, is troubled by a thought. Why should the Buddha's own Buddha-field be so impure? He even wonders whether it is because the Buddha's mind was impure when he created it. Reading his mind, the Buddha tells him that, just as the blind cannot see the sun and moon, however brightly they shine, so some beings cannot see the splendour of his Buddha-land due to their 'spiritual blindness', their ignorance. The Buddha-land is pure, but Śāriputra cannot see it.

The great god Śikhin then joins in the conversation, asserting that he himself sees the Buddha-land as equal in magnificence to the highest heavenly realms. Śāriputra replies that he sees it

> 'with its highs and lows, its thorns, its precipices, its peaks, and its abysses, as if it were entirely filled with ordure'.

Śikhin replies

> 'The fact that you see such a buddha-field as this as if it were so impure, reverend Śāriputra, is a sure sign that there are highs and lows in your mind and that your positive thought in regard to the buddha-gnosis is not pure either.'

As if to settle the matter, the Buddha touches the earth with his big toe, whereupon the whole universe is seen as a mass of sparkling jewels, and the entire assembly, including Śāriputra, perceive themselves to be seated on thrones of jewelled lotuses.[19]

The Buddha explains to Śāriputra that his Buddha-field is always as pure as it now appears

> 'but the Tathāgata makes it appear to be spoiled by many faults, in order to bring about the maturity of inferior living beings.'

Furthermore, he says that

> 'living beings born in the same buddha-field see the splendor of the virtues of the buddha-fields of the Buddhas according to their own degrees of purity.'

These two statements are, of course, contradictory. Do people see the purity or impurity of a Buddha-field because of how the Buddha makes it appear, or according to their own degree of purity? Both, the text would have us believe. In a way this contradiction runs throughout this particular aspect of the Mahāyāna. In the first case the Buddha-field objectively seems impure, and there is apparently no variation between the perceptions of the different beings who reside in it. To the extent that it is real as a creation, it really is an impure land. If it was unequivocally the case that the Pure Land consisted of the perception of the beings in it, that would imply that the Buddha creates the perceptions of other beings, which he does not. If he did, that would deprive them of all freedom and spiritual autonomy, whereas the implication of the second statement is that they have their own perceptions, which are not created by the Buddha.

It is a sort of koan, perhaps intentionally so. We should not try to explain the contradiction away; we need to meet it head on and admit that there is a contradiction. We should reflect on it and meditate on it from both points of view, and see whether that meditation results in a flash of Insight which enables us to reconcile the opposites, to rise above the contradiction. It may feel rather unsatisfactory not to be able to answer the question, but in fact it is deeply satisfying to find a real contradiction in a Mahāyāna text, a contradiction which cannot be resolved just by looking up one or two words in the *Buddhist Hybrid Sanskrit Dictionary*, but has to be meditated upon.

Having demonstrated the purity of the apparently 'impure' Buddha-field, the Buddha then returns the Buddha-field to its 'usual' state. As a result of all that has happened, the spiritual vision of large numbers of living beings is purified, and they attain varying degrees of realization. And so the first chapter ends.

It is possible that this chapter was originally a short separate work incorporated into the *Vimalakīrti-nirdeśa* at some point in its development. No more is heard of Ratnākara; and Vimalakīrti himself first appears at the beginning of the next chapter. Be that as it may, the chapter certainly constitutes an appropriate prologue to the main body of the text, setting the scene with its wonderful imagery and poetry, and its elements of magic and devotion.[20]

It also forms the background to the theme of the Buddha-land, which we will now consider in more detail. We have already seen what a Buddha-land is in terms of traditional Indian Buddhist cosmology. And we have also seen that the Buddha-land does not just appear. It is brought into being – built, even – by the Bodhisattva, who in the course of his own spiritual evolution sets up the ideal environment for the leading of the spiritual life. It is the Bodhisattva who 'purifies' the Buddha-land, as the text has it. Of course, a Buddha can create a Pure Land too, but generally it is a Bodhisattva who does so; and he does so in fulfilment of his vow to attain supreme perfect Enlightenment for the benefit of all living beings.

I have been referring to the Bodhisattva in the singular, but the text in fact suggests at several points that it is the Bodhisattvas – plural – who purify the Buddha-land. So why is this? Can a Bodhisattva not manage to build a Buddha-land on his own? Well, according to the Mahāyāna, an advanced Bodhisattva is quite capable of purifying or building the Buddha-land single-handed, just as a magician is capable of creating a magical elephant through his own power. But what would be the use?

Yes, you can create a Buddha-land and give people a glimpse of it. You may even be able to keep them in it for a little while. But you cannot keep them there indefinitely – not even if you are a Bodhisattva. This is because they are not going to co-operate, they are not going to want to stay there indefinitely, or even for very long, because they will not feel at home there. They are not ready for it.

There's a little Indian story that illustrates this point, and it will perhaps bring us down to earth somewhat, but never mind. The story is about a woman who sold fish. She lived in a small village on the banks of a big Indian river, and every week she took her fish to the market in a big basket. Now, one week, for some reason or other, it took her rather a long time to sell all her fish. She decided that rather than make her way back to the village so late at night, she had better stay in town. Fortunately she found a flower shop still open, and the flower-seller was sympathetic to her plight and said she could spend the night in his shop. Indian flower shops don't sell cut flowers in bunches as Western ones do; they sell sweet-smelling garlands, and little bunches of sweet-scented flowers for the ladies to put in their hair. The fish seller lay down to sleep among all those sweet-smelling flowers, but she tossed and turned, and couldn't get to sleep. She couldn't bear the scent of the flowers – they were so sweet, so beautiful. In the end, she got her old fish basket, which of course smelled strongly of fish, and put it right next to her, right by her nose. And after that, she slept quite soundly.

We might laugh at the fish-seller's plight, but we ourselves are in much the same position. She felt uncomfortable in the flower shop among all those sweet-smelling flowers; but we would feel no less uncomfortable in the Pure Land. We could manage a short visit, perhaps a weekend, but eventually we would want to introduce some equivalent of her smelly old fish basket into the Pure Land. We would want to bring along some physical or mental distraction – perhaps our television set, our motor bike, our record collection, our lover, or our office files. Then we would feel more comfortable, more at home. But then, of course, the Pure Land would no longer be the Pure Land.

So the Bodhisattva cannot keep people in the Buddha-land against their will. In any case, that would be a contradiction in terms, because the spiritual life is essentially the autonomous life, the free life, the emancipated life. So what is the Bodhisattva to do? He cannot create a Buddha-land by magical power and then hold people in it – at least, not for very long. They will soon start getting uncomfortable, and then – no more Buddha-land.

The answer is that the Buddha-land has to be a joint creation. It has to be built by a number of people – Bodhisattvas and would-be Bodhisattvas – working together. One of them may be more advanced than the others, may have more vision, may even be the first to attain Enlightenment and then help the others to take that final step. But all must be inspired by the same ideal, the ideal of supreme perfect Enlightenment for the benefit of all beings. They all therefore follow the Bodhisattva path, follow it for thousands of lives – and all follow it together. This is a truly wonderful conception: the whole spiritual community being reborn together as a spiritual community, living and working together, helping one another, life after life, until the Buddha-land is established.

There is some reflection of this idea in the Pali Jātaka stories, in which the Buddha's disciples – Ānanda, Yaśodharā, Sāriputta, Mahākassapa, even Devadatta – are represented as having been associated with him in many previous existences. On a more mundane level, a remarkable book was published in England a few years ago telling the story of a group of Cathars in southern France in the thirteenth century who were said to have been reborn during the Napoleonic wars, and again in the present century in Cornwall. In all these different lives they have been in personal contact with one another, and have tried to help one another in their development.[21]

But why does the Bodhisattva – why do the Bodhisattvas – build the Buddha-land? It would be easy to answer this question along straightforward traditional lines. We could say that the Bodhisattva wants to help others by providing them with an ideal environment in which to develop spiritually. This is quite correct as far as it goes, but it only raises a further question. Why should the Bodhisattva be concerned with others at all?

To answer this we have to go a little deeper. Should we devote ourselves to our own emancipation or to helping others? This question is crucial to the spiritual life. In the context of Buddhism it amounts to asking whether we should follow the Arhant ideal or the Bodhisattva ideal – envisaging these two ideals in their extreme, even mutually exclusive, forms.

In its extreme form, the Arhant ideal is to gain emancipation for oneself alone without bothering too much about other people. The Bodhisattva ideal, on the contrary, is to help others to become free without bothering too much about oneself. But the two ideals are not as contradictory as they may seem. Indeed, they cannot really be separated. You cannot really help yourself without helping others, and you cannot really help others without helping yourself.

We are social beings. (I won't say '*essentially* social beings' as this could be misunderstood to suggest that we have to have a 'social life'.) It is impossible to cut yourself off from other people for any length of time, even though you may cut yourself off from physical contact with them. You influence them; they influence you. If you develop emotional positivity, imagination, and insight within yourself, that has its effect on others; and if you work for others, give to others, sacrifice yourself for them, that has its effect on you.

So we cannot really separate helping ourselves from helping others, certainly not in the spiritual sphere. The Arhant ideal and the Bodhisattva ideal are inseparable. Carried to their logical conclusion, each includes the other. The Bodhisattvas build the Buddha-land because they have no alternative. If you want to evolve spiritually, you have to evolve in free association with others. Blake says: 'Mutual forgiveness of each vice: Such are the gates of paradise.'[22] Similarly – though less poetically – we could say: 'Mutual helpfulness in leading the spiritual life: such is the foundation of the Buddha-land.'

And what do the Bodhisattvas use to build the Buddha-land? The Buddha himself answers this question in his reply to Ratnākara: 'A buddha-field of bodhisattvas is a field of living beings.' In other words, a Buddha-land is built with living beings – that is, with living beings who want to evolve. As Hakuin says in his 'Song of Meditation': 'Outside living beings, no Buddhas.' No living beings, no Buddha-land. In short, if you want to build a Buddha-land, you need people. In a sense, in fact, people are all that you need. It doesn't matter if you don't have buildings or money. If you have got people, you have got everything. And if you haven't got people, you haven't got anything.

This is true not only in building the Buddha-land, but at all levels of the spiritual life. If you want to have a spiritual community or a spiritual movement, you need people. If you want to hold a retreat or give a talk on Buddhism, you need people. It is not enough to have the facilities, not enough to have the teacher or the speaker. You need people – people who want to become true individuals, people who want to evolve.

At the same time, we should not take this metaphor too literally. The Bodhisattva is not a sort of spiritual bricklayer, fitting people neatly into place with the aid of a bit of compassion for cement. People are not passive; people are not inert; people are not things. A Bodhisattva can build the Buddha-land with people only with their co-operation – and co-operation means communication. So there is no question of the Bodhisattvas literally building the Buddha-land with other people. In helping to build the Buddha-land, the 'other people' are themselves aspiring Bodhisattvas – so the Bodhisattvas really build the Buddha-land with themselves.

As to how the Bodhisattvas build the Buddha-land, the Buddha answers this question too, when he says that a Bodhisattva's Buddha-field is a field of positive thought, a field of high resolve, a field of virtuous application, a field of the six perfections, a field of the four immeasurables (friendliness, compassion, joy, and equanimity), a field of the ten precepts, and so on. Bodhisattvas build a Buddha-field to the extent that they develop themselves spiritually, to the extent that they practise the Dharma for the benefit of all. They purify a Buddha-field to the extent that they purify their own minds. Notice that the Buddha speaks of *a* Bodhisattva here. This reminds us that the Dharma is to be practised by each of us individually, even though we practise in spiritual fellowship with others who are also practising. The Buddha-land is built by the Bodhisattvas' united but individual practice of the Dharma.

We have seen that the Buddha-land is the ideal environment – envisaged on a cosmic scale – for the leading of the spiritual life. It is built by the united spiritual efforts of the Bodhisattvas, and they build it because, if they want to be Bodhisattvas at all, they have no choice. The spiritual development of one of them involves the spiritual development of all, and vice versa. The Bodhisattvas build the Buddha-land with their own lives and by means of their individual practice of the Dharma within a context of spiritual fellowship.

But in a way this doesn't help us very much. It only leads to an even bigger question: what has all this to do with us? All the magic and splendour, all the deep metaphysical ideas, all the colour of this Mahāyāna sūtra: what has it to do with us? What have we to do with building the Buddha-land? A Buddha-land is, after all, something we can hardly imagine. It is built mainly by advanced Bodhisattvas, beings we can hardly imagine, by means of a practice of the Dharma we can hardly imagine. So what has it all got to do with us?

To answer this question we have to come right down to earth. Or rather, we have only to come some way down to earth, because the question may be addressed, at least indirectly, by considering a field of human activity which, we may say, mediates between the world of higher spiritual values and mundane, everyday existence. This is the field of art and creativity.

One often hears people saying – sometimes apologetically, sometimes defiantly, sometimes wistfully, sometimes ironically – 'I'm not very creative.' What they usually mean by this is that they cannot paint pictures, write poetry, compose music, or throw pots. Artistic creativity seems to be in vogue these days; everyone is supposed to be creative. But what do we mean by being creative? Is it just a matter of being able to paint pictures?

Creativity involves a distinction between subject and object. On the one hand there is you, the artist; on the other, the material out of which you create your work of art, as well as the 'idea' in accordance with which you create it, an idea that may be more or less conscious. And the 'material' out of which the artist creates may be of several kinds. There's the obvious physical stuff out of which a work is made – clay, paint, sound, language, or whatever. Then there's the involvement of the artist's own person: the voice, the physical body, the mental and emotional states. And other people also become 'artistic material', either as merely passive material for the artist's creativity (like a sculptor's model), or actively co-operating with it, themselves creative in relation to the artist's creativity (like an orchestra or a cast of actors). In the latter case, there is no absolute distinction between the artist and the 'material' – the people – from which they create.

Generally we experience ourselves as subjects in relation to the 'object' of the whole external world in the broadest sense. But we are not passive in relation to the external world. We do not merely register impressions. The world impinges on us, and we also impinge on the world, on our own environment, or a part of it. We impinge on our own selves, on ourselves considered as objects to ourselves (that is, considered reflexively), and we also impinge on other people. Not only do we impinge on the world; we affect it in various ways. We alter it, we arrange it, we *re*-arrange it – at least to some extent, however slight. And not only that. There is a pattern to the way in which we impinge on the world. We don't impinge on it at random, but in accordance with a certain idea, a certain pattern, image, gestalt, or myth, within ourselves – even, we could say, a pattern which *is* ourselves.

It is rare for us consciously to realize this, but what it means is that our relationship with the world is essentially creative. We are creating all the time. Creativity is not limited to the exercise of the fine arts; everyone is creative. It is only a question of the quality of our creativity – greater or lesser success, greater or lesser clarity, greater or lesser positivity. We are creative when we speak, when we decorate a room, when we write a letter. This is the basic principle of what we may call 'applied Zen' – Zen applied to the art of living itself.

Zen is a well-known example of the application of spiritual realization to various otherwise mundane activities in such a way as to bring them into harmony with that realization. In this way, Zen is applied to architecture, to landscape gardening, to archery or swordsmanship, to flower arrangement, and to everyday manners and customs. The Zen approach, in which the human subject is creative in relation to its object, is akin to the building of the Buddha-land, in that it transforms various aspects of the world.

The extent to which it is possible to bring about such a transformation will depend on all sorts of factors: the material resources that are available to you, the nature of the environment, the degree of co-operation that you get from other people, and so on. Suppose, for instance, you want to apply the principle of Zen to the surrounding landscape. It doesn't depend just on your own personal inspiration or realization; you need the co-operation of other people, because they have as much responsibility for the environment as you. But in principle there is no reason why it shouldn't be possible to express your creativity in this large-scale way. It depends not only on how deep your meditation practice is, but on other quite mundane factors, even on worldly power. In the past, kings and emperors who have been sympathetic to Ch'an or Zen have been able to order the construction of many Zen-type gardens and buildings.

It is not, either, that your creativity always needs to take a particular kind of formal expression, but it always takes *some* kind of formal expression. The expression has to take a particular form, whether it be that of painting or poetry, architecture or landscape gardening, archery or flower arranging. If you don't have the power to construct a Zen temple, you can at least paint your room, or even just tidy it up. The way you eat your food, the way you set out your dishes, even the way you do the washing-up – all these can be the application of Zen to the art of living.

Art is a particularly appropriate analogy for the creation of a Buddha-land because it involves giving a harmonious external embodiment to an idea, which is what, in a very much higher sense, a Buddha or a Bodhisattva does when he sets about building a Buddha-land. A Buddha-land is a sort of work of art. But the principle operates in everyone's life all the time, not just in the life of the artist, because all the time we all have an influence on our environment; we interact with the world, and that interaction can be negative and destructive or positive and creative. It is the positive, creative kind of interaction with the world to which especially we give the name 'art'.

Another close analogy to building a Buddha-land is the 'art' of statesmanship. The laying down of laws which make possible the development of a positive and harmonious society is certainly one of the arts in the broader sense in which we have defined the term. The lawgiver impinges on the world in accordance with a certain idea, a certain pattern, which he usually quite consciously realizes. One could therefore regard great statesmen and leaders as being essentially creative or as exercising a specifically creative function.

In most cases throughout history 'the masses' have been relatively passive, and their leaders have just issued orders sanctioned by force and fear. These situations have not therefore given the statesmen the opportunity to practise the highest form of such creativity. You could practise this only if you could enlist people's willing co-operation in the formation and enactment of laws and the creation of the kind of society that those laws made possible. Statesmen – whether individually or collectively – can certainly change society. Whether they change it positively or in a genuinely creative manner, is, of course, quite a different question. But we could speak of Zen and the art of statesmanship.

In Buddhist tradition, the *cakravartin-rāja*, the 'wheel-turning king', is ranked second only to the Buddha. Had the Buddha himself not decided to become a Buddha, tradition has it that he would have become a *cakravartin-rāja*. We are told quite specifically that the principal function of a *cakravartin-rāja* is to create or maintain a society in which the ten *akuśala-dharmas* are banished and the practice of the ten *kuśala-dharmas* (ten precepts) is encouraged. We could say that the Buddha works on a restricted section of society, primarily on the Sangha; but the *cakravartin-rāja* works on society as a whole – without of course being Enlightened in the way that the Buddha is.

We should not, however, confuse the essentially mundane activity of the *cakravartin-rāja* with, say, Amitābha's creation of Sukhāvatī. At the very least, Sukhāvatī is a transfigured material world, whereas the world of the *cakravartin-rāja* is definitely the ordinary, workaday world of society, economics, politics, ethics, and so on: the world of government in the ordinary sense. But the ruler performs essentially the same function, or engages in essentially the same type of activity, as the artist. His task may be more difficult, because he is having to deal with human beings rather than inert materials. It is comparatively easy to manipulate pigments and marble and words; but to create a particular kind of society by organizing the activities of human beings without restricting their freedom is extremely difficult. In fact, you would have to be something of a saint to succeed. People sometimes complain about organizations and the state without really considering what a difficult task government must be.

Ideally, of course, there would be no need for government, because we would all take responsibility for ourselves. If our relation to the world is essentially creative, the notable conclusion that follows is that the world – *our* world – is our creation. We create the world we live in. There is no question, therefore, of whether or not we should be creative, of whether or not we should create a world. We have no choice. The only choice we have is what kind of world we create.

The Tibetan Wheel of Life depicts six realms of existence which illustrate the kinds of worlds we can create for ourselves. We can create a world of the gods, a world of refined, sensuous, intellectual, aesthetic, but rather selfish, self-indulgent pleasure; or a world of human beings, a world of ordinary domestic, civic, political, and cultural obligations and activities. We can create a world of *āsuras* or anti-gods, a world of jealousy, excessive sexual polarization, over-aggressiveness, ruthless competition, and overt or covert conflict; or a world of hungry ghosts, a world of neurotic craving, intense possessiveness, and relationships characterized by extreme emotional dependence. We can create a world of tormented beings, a world of pain and suffering, of intense physical and mental distress; or a world of animals, a world of straightforward food, sex, and sleep.

Or, turning our back on all these, we can devote ourselves to developing as individuals. We can devote ourselves to the Bodhisattva ideal. We can devote ourselves, directly or indirectly, to building the Buddha-land.

But we need not feel bound to choose any of these worlds. There is another option open to us. Turning our back on the Wheel of Life altogether, we can begin to tread the Spiral Path that leads to Enlightenment. We can devote ourselves to developing as individuals, to the Bodhisattva ideal. And in so doing, we choose to create another kind of world. In other words, we devote ourselves, directly or indirectly, to building the Buddha-land.

3

On Being 'All Things to All Men'

Over the past nearly four hundred years, the Authorized Version of the Bible has had a great influence on the English language, and many people still relish its turn of phrase. Being 'all things to all men' is an expression taken from the New Testament, from one of the letters of the apostle Paul to the Christians of the various cities he visited in the course of his travels. In several of these epistles, Paul refers to problems or disputes within those early Christian communities. Reading between the lines of his first letter to the Corinthians, one gets the impression that he feels he has to defend himself against some criticism. We find him saying, apparently by way of justification, that he has made himself every man's servant, to win over as many people as possible. To win over the Jews he has become like a Jew; to win over the Gentiles, the heathen, he has become like a Gentile. In short, he says, he has become 'all things to all men, that I might by all means save some'.[23] His strategy, in other words, is to relate to everybody on their own terms.

Being 'all things to all men' is what the Bodhisattva Vimalakīrti excels at. The second chapter of the *Vimalakīrti-nirdeśa* introduces him to us:

> He was liberated through the transcendence of wisdom. Having integrated his realization with skill in liberative technique, he was

> expert in knowing the thoughts and actions of living beings. Knowing the strength or weakness of their faculties, and being gifted with unrivaled eloquence, he taught the Dharma appropriately to each. Having applied himself energetically to the Mahāyāna, he understood it and accomplished his tasks with great finesse. He lived with the deportment of a Buddha, and his superior intelligence was as wide as an ocean. He was praised, honored, and commended by all the Buddhas and was respected by Indra, Brahmā, and all the Lokapālas. In order to develop living beings with his skill in liberative technique, he lived in the great city of Vaiśālī.[24]

The text goes on to describe Vimalakīrti's practice of the six *pāramitās*, the six 'perfections' of the Bodhisattva: generosity, morality, patience, vigour, meditation, and wisdom:

> His wealth was inexhaustible for the purpose of sustaining the poor and the helpless. He observed a pure morality in order to protect the immoral. He maintained tolerance and self-control in order to reconcile beings who were angry, cruel, violent, and brutal. He blazed with energy in order to inspire people who were lazy. He maintained concentration, mindfulness, and meditation in order to sustain the mentally troubled. He attained decisive wisdom in order to sustain the foolish.

We are then given a vivid picture of his way of life:

> He wore the white clothes of the layman, yet lived impeccably like a religious devotee. He lived at home, but remained aloof from the realm of desire, the realm of pure matter, and the immaterial realm. He had a son, a wife, and female attendants, yet always maintained continence. He appeared to be surrounded by servants, yet lived in solitude. He appeared to be adorned with ornaments, yet always was endowed with the auspicious signs and marks. He seemed to eat and drink, yet always took nourishment from the taste of meditation. He made his appearance at the fields of sports and in the casinos, but his aim was always to mature those people who were attached to games and gambling. He visited the fashionable heterodox teachers, yet always kept unswerving loyalty to the Buddha. He understood the mundane and transcendental sciences and esoteric practices, yet always took pleasure in the delights of the Dharma. He mixed in all crowds, yet was respected as foremost of all.
>
> In order to be in harmony with people, he associated with elders,

> with those of middle age, and with the young, yet always spoke in harmony with the Dharma. He engaged in all sorts of businesses, yet had no interest in profit or possessions. To train living beings, he would appear at crossroads and on street corners, and to protect them he participated in government. To turn people away from the Hīnayāna and to engage them in the Mahāyāna, he appeared among listeners and teachers of the Dharma. To develop children, he visited all the schools. To demonstrate the evils of desire, he even entered the brothels. To establish drunkards in correct mindfulness, he entered all the cabarets.

So as he went about living his life in the great city of Vaiśālī, Vimalakīrti met everybody at their own level, in their own environment, and on their own ground. This is why I would suggest that Vimalakīrti was 'all things to all men'. This quality of being able to relate to people on their own terms is technically known as *upāya-kauśalya*, 'skilful means' or, as here, 'liberative technique', and the Mahāyāna attached such great importance to it that it came to be considered the seventh *pāramitā*, a seventh perfection for the Bodhisattva to cultivate as well as the usual six.[25]

But why does Mahāyāna Buddhism hold skilful means in such high regard? To answer this, we need to consider again the situation of a Bodhisattva creating a Buddha-land. We have seen that a Bodhisattva may magically create a Pure Land – either literally or metaphorically – but even a Bodhisattva cannot force people to stay in it if they do not feel at home there. The Pure Land has to be a joint creation, built by a number of Bodhisattvas working together, a community of people inspired by the same ideal, the ideal of supreme perfect Enlightenment for the benefit of all.

Similarly, the Bodhisattva, however sincere and well-intentioned, is not going to get very far if he approaches everybody in the same way or speaks to everybody in the same language – least of all if he tries to speak to them as a Bodhisattva. People, as we realize more and more the older we get, are very diverse indeed. We all have our different backgrounds, our different conditioning. We have our different ways of looking at things, our different attitudes. We live in different circumstances, and we pursue different occupations and interests. We have different tastes and prejudices, and even different virtues.

To be effective – and a Bodhisattva who is not effective is not a Bodhisattva at all – the Bodhisattva has to take all this into account. To communicate with people, you have to speak to them in their own language, literally and metaphorically. More than that: to be able to speak to them at all, you first have to establish contact with them. And to do that, you have to appear like one of them. You have to be 'all things to all men'. Vimalakīrti exemplifies this to a greater degree than any other figure in Mahāyāna Buddhist literature, with the possible exception of the Buddha himself. He appears among businessmen as a businessman; among government officials as a government official; among warriors as a warrior. Above all, he appears among laymen as a layman. Vimalakīrti's status as a layman has, however, led to some serious misunderstandings, which we will be looking at later in this chapter.

In reality, of course, he is quite different from other people; he is an advanced Bodhisattva. But he doesn't make a point of being different; he doesn't insist on it. He doesn't appear among people proclaiming that he is an advanced Bodhisattva, wearing his Bodhisattva gear. He doesn't always have to appear nodding his three heads or waving his four arms, although this is very often the sort of thing people expect. They think that someone who is spiritually advanced will appear different from others in an obvious, striking, even peculiar or eccentric way.

Many years ago in Calcutta I got to know a religiously-minded Bengali lady. One day she told me that when she was a little girl, about seven or eight, her mother took her to see the 'Holy Mother', Sarada Devi. Sarada Devi was the consort of the famous Bengali mystic Sri Ramakrishna. She outlived him by many years, and was believed to be a very spiritually advanced person in her own right. My friend's mother told her that they were going to see a real *devi*. Now, in Indian languages the term *devi* generally means 'a lady', but it can also mean 'a goddess' or 'a spiritual woman'. So the little girl got very excited. She had heard and read so much about *devis*, but so far she had only seen images of them in the temples. Now she was going to see a real goddess at last, and she was looking forward to seeing a larger than life figure, probably breathing fire, and almost certainly having at least eight arms. When they got home from the visit, however, she complained bitterly to her mother. She said 'You told me that we were going to see a real goddess, but all we saw was a little old lady in a white sari!'

Like the little girl, we are often unable to appreciate the fact that someone is spiritually advanced if they look more or less like anyone else. But this is how the Bodhisattva appears. At the same time, just as he doesn't make a point of being different, he doesn't make a point of being like other people either. He doesn't act 'ordinary' in a self-conscious way. He is not like a liberal Christian clergyman who takes off his dog-collar, goes along to the local pub, and tries to behave like 'one of the lads'. The

Bodhisattva doesn't go around earnestly assuring people that he is just like everybody else.

The Bodhisattva is simply himself. On the one hand, he doesn't behave in a special Bodhisattva-like manner; on the other hand, he doesn't pretend to be ordinary. He *is* ordinary; but at the same time, he *is* a Bodhisattva. He is himself. And because he can be himself, he can approach people and communicate with them in a natural, unselfconscious way.

The Bodhisattva does not use a special technique – not even a 'liberative technique', which is how Thurman translates *upāya-kauśalya*. In his notes, Thurman says that he has chosen the word 'technique' in preference to the more usual 'method' or 'means' because it has a stronger connotation of efficacy in our technological world. This may be so, but I can't help wondering whether it connotes the right sort of efficacy in this particular context. It makes it sound as though the Bodhisattva has some sort of trick up his sleeve, or as though he tries to 'win friends and influence people' in a rather slick, artificial way. Even the words 'method' and 'means' have that sort of connotation to some extent. But *upāya-kauśalya* is essentially a matter of being able to be with people, of empathizing with them, encouraging them to be open with you and to you. This is why the Mahāyāna attaches great importance to skilful means.

The Hīnayāna does not emphasize skilful means in this way; the term *upāya-kauśalya* occurs only once in the Pali canon as far as I know, and that is in the ordinary sense of a trick. So, although we can see the Buddha exercising this virtue in various ways – for instance, with Kisā-Gotamī[26] – it is not named as such till we come to the Mahāyāna.

Skilful means, as the Mahāyāna sees it, has a broader meaning, in fact, than simply acting in a way that encourages people to be open with you. It can even include actions which appear to be unethical but which are in fact highly ethical on account of the underlying motivation; indeed, such actions could be said to be examples *par excellence* of *upāya-kauśalya*, because you are being so very skilful that you use even an apparently unethical action to fulfil a spiritual purpose.

This, of course, does not take account of what third parties might think of what you are doing. What makes the *upāya-kauśalya* skilful is its effect on the person towards whom it is directed. If it fulfils its purpose in an apparently unethical manner, it is more skilful than ever. But the Bodhisattva has to take into account all the sentient beings in the environment, so he does have to consider the possible effects of his skilful means on observers. Having done this, he may decide to go ahead with the apparently unethical action for the benefit of the person towards whom it is directed, or he may not. But whatever he does, it will be a skilful means. He may, through supernormal powers, be able to make his action invisible to those who are not directly involved with it.

In the parable of the burning house in the *White Lotus Sūtra*, we find that the Buddha appears to feel he has to justify his action in promising the children three different kinds of cart when he knew that he was only going to give them one kind. He has to explain that he has not really told a lie. The reason he has to spell it out is that at the time the *White Lotus Sūtra* was produced, the term *upāya-kauśalya* apparently had an ambiguous meaning; perhaps the specifically Mahayanic sense of the term had not been definitely established. This is speculation; but certainly in that parable the Buddha appears very conscious of the fact that his skilful means could be regarded as just ordinary trickery. But eventually *upāya-kauśalya* came to mean skilful means in a purely spiritual sense.

Sometimes people use the term 'skilful means' as a rationalization for unskilful behaviour; this is of course to be avoided. We should use the term *upāya-kauśalya* only when we are talking about *upāya-kauśalya*, not when we are talking about our own weaknesses or mistakes. For instance, if in the course of discussion you become very angry with someone and lose your temper, you may say afterwards 'I'm sure it did him good – so I guess that was just my skilful means.' But really you are fooling yourself. We should be careful not to use the expression 'skilful means' as a euphemism for tricky behaviour; that debases the whole idea.

Very often disciples rationalize the dubious activities of their spiritual teachers in this way, and insist on regarding questionable behaviour on the part of the so-called teacher as being his 'skilful means'. They do this, presumably, because they need to keep up their 'faith' in their teacher. They say 'he could not have been angry' because they need to believe that he could not possibly ever get angry. One does find, particularly among some Western followers of Tibetan Buddhism, this very rigid belief – one can't call it faith in the real sense – in the integrity of their teachers which they are just not prepared to question or examine at all.

Traditionally, Mahāyāna Buddhism holds that the practice of skilful means consists essentially in three things: first of all, the four *saṁgraha-vastus* or 'elements of conversion'; secondly, the four *pratisaṁvids* or 'analytical knowledges'; and thirdly, the *dhāraṇīs* or 'magical formulae'. We will go into each of these in turn; between them, they give a good idea of what skilful means is really about.

(1) The Four *Saṁgrahavastus* or 'Elements of Conversion'

'Elements of conversion' is the usual translation, but Thurman has suggested an alternative that brings out the real meaning of the term: 'means of unification'. Unification here is the unification of the spiritual community, or, as Thurman explains it, 'the four ways in which a bodhisattva forms a group of people united by their common aim of practising the Dharma'.[27] The point here is that the Bodhisattva's aim in using skilful means – in being himself the skilful means – is not just to lead people to Enlightenment individually, but to enlist their co-operation in building the Buddha-land for the benefit of all.

(a) Dāna: 'Giving' or 'Generosity'

The first means of unification is that most basic of Buddhist virtues, *dāna* or giving. It is perhaps surprising to find *dāna* included as part of the seventh *pāramitā*; after all, it has a whole *pāramitā* to itself – *dāna* is the first *pāramitā*. But here it has a special function. In this context it is a means of establishing positive contact between people, of creating spiritual friendship, of helping to form a spiritual community.

We usually think of *dāna* in a more utilitarian way; we tend to give people something because they need it. But *dāna* in this context is not quite like that; at least, not in a narrow sense. You give people things because you like them, because you want to be spiritual friends with them, because you want to form a spiritual community with them. Not, of course, that you give in a calculating way, to bring about those particular results. The whole process is completely natural, completely spontaneous. By giving someone a present, you give expression to your special awareness of them, your positive feeling towards them, your special concern for them. Giving is in fact a form of communication.

We could even say, as a general principle, that a spiritual community is characterized by the constant exchange of presents among its members. The exchange of presents strengthens the spiritual community. It is, indeed, a natural expression of the life of the spiritual community. These gifts are not given 'in return' for anything. You just naturally feel like giving to one another, and you express that feeling by the giving of gifts.

(b) Priya-vāditā: 'Loving Speech'

The second means of unification is another familiar quality among all those that the Buddhist seeks to develop: *priya-vāditā* or *priya-vacana* is enumerated as an aspect of Perfect Speech, the third limb of the Noble Eightfold Path.[28] *Priya* can also be rendered as 'affectionate', 'pleasing', or 'pleasant'. The Bodhisattva establishes contact with people by speaking to them in an emotionally positive – that is, kindly – manner. Affectionate speech is therefore the rule within the spiritual community, among those who are engaged in building the Buddha-land. A Bodhisattva is not afraid of giving expression to affection for others, or of letting other people know that he likes them. He is not even afraid of telling them to their face that he likes them – just in case there is any doubt about it. After all, some people find it difficult to believe that anybody actually likes them. It may even come as quite a shock. But it's important to understand what is really meant by affectionate speech. It doesn't necessarily involve going around addressing everybody as 'dear' or 'darling'. There's nothing wrong with terms of endearment as such – but I remember hearing a snippet from some drama on the radio and an American character saying 'I'm going to kill you right now, darling.'

The word *priya* usually means 'love' or 'affection' in quite an ordinary sense. But here *priya-vāditā* is being practised by the Bodhisattva as a means of helping to create the spiritual community, as an aspect of the seventh *pāramitā*, *upāya*. And the *pāramitā* which precedes *upāya* is *prajñā*, wisdom. It follows that for the Bodhisattva 'loving speech' is an expression of transcendental wisdom. The love to which the Bodhisattva gives verbal expression is not just love in the ordinary sense. It is not ordinary human affection or friendliness, still less sexual attraction or sentimentality or even plain gregariousness. In this context, love is an expression of spiritual insight, of the Bodhisattva's delighted awareness of people's spiritual potential.

(c) Artha-caryā: 'Beneficial Activity'

The third means of unification is *artha-caryā*. *Artha-caryā* can be translated as 'beneficial activity' – that is, activity for the benefit of others – but it literally means 'doing good'. This is not at all to suggest that the Bodhisattva is some kind of professional 'do-gooder', doing to people what he thinks will be good for them. Once again we have to look at the context. *Artha-caryā* doesn't mean doing merely what is of benefit in an ordinary, everyday, worldly sense. It means doing whatever helps people spiritually, whatever helps them to attain higher and ever higher levels of being and consciousness. The Bodhisattva practises beneficial activity by sharing with people his own experience of the Dharma, sharing with them – in a word – himself.

This is not a matter of teaching the Dharma in the way that you might teach history or arithmetic. It is not simply a question of imparting information, although that may be involved. The Bodhisattva teaches people by encouraging them to grow and develop. It has been said that inspiration is the single most important factor in the whole of the spiritual life. You may have all the information you need, you may have all the facilities and opportunities, but if you don't have inspiration, you are not going to get very far. So the Bodhisattva benefits people by inspiring them, by sparking them off; by communicating to them the emotional positivity, the creativity, and the excitement, the sheer adventure, of the spiritual life. The Bodhisattva is like a candle which lights thousands upon thousands of other candles – after which they go on burning on their own fuel. Not only that: all of them in their turn light thousands upon thousands of other candles.

(d) Samānārthata: 'Exemplification'

The fourth means of unification is exemplification. In other words, the Bodhisattva's behaviour is consistent with his teaching. His teaching is the Dharma and his behaviour exemplifies his teaching. In a time-honoured phrase, he practises what he preaches (except, of course, that he doesn't preach). The Bodhisattva is the living embodiment of all the qualities that he encourages others to develop. He inspires people to lead the spiritual life because he himself is inspired.

Here a difficulty arises – not so much for the Bodhisattva, but for those of us who are still trying to become Bodhisattvas. We may have a vision of the ideal, a vision of spiritual perfection, even a vision of the Buddha-land, but we cannot live up to it. Sometimes, in fact, we fall very far short of it indeed. We sincerely believe in it, we are inspired by it, but we find it very difficult to transform our lives in accordance with it. In other words, we come up against that well-known divide between the Path of Vision and the Path of Transformation.[29]

But the discrepancy we feel between our vision and our ability to live in accordance with it need not prevent us from trying to communicate that vision. All that we really have to communicate – all that we *can* communicate – is ourselves. The key is simply to be as honest as possible. We can feel free to talk as much as we like about our vision and our efforts to transform ourselves in accordance with it. We can rejoice in our successes and, if necessary, confess our failures. We need not be afraid to be honest; we need not hold back because our practice is 'not good enough'.

In any case, the Buddhist vision is not of some fixed and finite goal. It is a vision of constant transformation, of ever-increasing creativity with no perceptible limit. When we exemplify our vision, this is what we really exemplify. Exemplification does not mean embodying a particular static point in the process of spiritual development, however high that point may be. It means embodying the process of spiritual development itself, to however limited an extent. What is going to come across is that, whatever point we have reached so far, we are truly making an effort to evolve.

(2) The Four *Pratisaṁvids* or 'Analytical Knowledges'

The four *pratisaṁvids* are the second group of qualities in which the practice of skilful means consists. Like the *saṁgrahavastus,* they were taken over by the Mahāyāna from the Hīnayāna, and in taking them over the Mahāyāna modified their meaning in accordance with its own rather more altruistic outlook. 'Knowledges' is not really a very satisfactory translation, as one of these four items is not a knowledge in the ordinary sense at all, and 'infallible penetrations', another often-used translation, does not help us much either. We can only really get some idea of the nature of the *pratisaṁvids* by going into them a little.

(a) Dharma-pratisaṁvid: 'Analytical Knowledge of Phenomena'

We need not take the idea of 'knowledge of phenomena' too seriously; another possible translation is 'analytical knowledge of principles'. It consists in the realization of the truth or the reality of things independent of any words or conceptual formulations. This is possible only if one has gone beyond words and conceptual formulations, only if one is personally in contact with the truth and reality of things.

According to the *Daśabhūmika Sūtra, dharma-pratisaṁvid* includes knowledge of how the different paths or *yānas* of the Buddhist tradition merge together. Essentially the *yānas* are formulations of the Buddha's teachings in accordance with the needs of different kinds of people; in other words, the *yānas* themselves are skilful means. They all eventually meet together in one *yāna* because they are all concerned in one way or another with the same thing, with the spiritual development of the individual. The more individuals develop, the more they realize their unity with one another; and the more they realize their unity with one another, the more they realize that they are all following the same path. This idea of the *ekayāna,* the 'one way', is one of the fundamental teachings of another important Mahāyāna text, the *White Lotus Sūtra.*[30]

(b) Artha-pratisaṁvid: 'Analytical Knowledge of Meaning'

One might think that realization of the truth or reality of things is a considerable achievement – but it is not enough for the Bodhisattva. The four analytical knowledges are all part of the seventh *pāramitā*, the perfection of skilful means; so the Bodhisattva is going to want to communicate the truth or reality of things to other people, in the interests of their growth and development.

And if you want to communicate, you need a medium of communication. To begin with, you need a common rational framework. In Buddhism this is provided by the conceptual formulations of the teachings: the Four Noble Truths, the Noble Eightfold Path, the Five Spiritual Faculties, and so on. In other words, it is provided by what may be called the philosophy of Buddhism. (It is also provided by the various things which the Bodhisattva creates by means of his magical power, but we are not concerned with that aspect of the matter at present.) Thus *artha-pratisaṁvid* consists in knowledge of the conceptual formulations of the teaching, not just on their own conceptual level, nor for their own sake, but as a medium for communicating the truth or reality of things, a medium for communicating spiritual values.

(c) Nirukti-pratisaṁvid: 'Analytical Knowledge of Etymology'

Surely this is a rather strange, not to say academic, accomplishment for a Bodhisattva to bother acquiring – a knowledge of the origin and derivation of words? Well, not really. We have seen that knowledge of the truth and reality of things is not enough. We have seen that the Bodhisattva wants to communicate, so he needs the 'analytical knowledge of meaning', that is, knowledge of the meaning of the conceptual formulations of the teaching. But even this is not enough. The Bodhisattva needs to be able to give expression to his understanding of those conceptual formulations in words – and for that, he must know precisely what the words mean.

Only too often our communication is limited by our vagueness about the meaning of the words we use. We tend to fall back on a limited number of expressions which constant repetition has rendered almost meaningless. Speaking in clichés is really little better than grunting or squeaking. We therefore need to know what words mean – not just in the dictionary sense, although that is not to be despised. Just as concepts need to be related back to the experience of reality which they formulate, so words need to be related back to the concepts of which they are the expression. And it is in this that the Bodhisattva's analytical knowledge of etymology essentially consists. The Bodhisattva is never misled by words. He is never carried away by words. He never gets lost in words. He uses words to express concepts, clear concepts, just as he uses concepts to formulate spiritual experiences, spiritual realities.

Nirukti-pratisaṁvid also includes knowledge of such things as linguistics, public speaking, and literary composition, all of which are traditionally associated with the figure of Mañjuśrī or Mañjughoṣa, the Bodhisattva of Wisdom. In fact, he is the embodiment of all four analytical knowledges. The colophon of the Mañjughoṣa Stūti Sādhana ends with these words: 'And through this [practice] may all living beings gain power in the *jñāna* of the four *pratisaṁvids*.' We could hardly find a clearer emphasis of the importance of the four *pratisaṁvids* to the Bodhisattva's practice of skilful means.

(d) Pratibhāna-pratisaṁvid: 'Analytical Knowledge of Courage'

You may have personal experience of the truth and reality of things, at least to some extent. You may have conceptual formulations of that experience clearly in your mind. You may even have the words with which to express those conceptual formulations. But all that is not enough. There is still something else you need if you are going to communicate effectively: courage. It is not enough to know the words. You must be able to find them – and the courage to say them – at the very moment they are needed. You need boldness, promptitude, wit. The words – and the courage – are no use a week or a day or even an hour later. It may be poor memory that prevents us from finding the right words when we need them, but often it is simply lack of confidence in ourselves and in what we have to communicate. So as part of *upāya-pāramitā* the Bodhisattva also cultivates the 'analytical knowledge' of courage, the courage to speak out when necessary.

It is perhaps sobering to consider the contrast between the Bodhisattva's practice of the *pratisaṁvids* and our own efforts in this area. To begin with, most of us have little or no experience of the truth or reality of things. And our conceptual formulations, our ideas, are more often than not vague, confused, and unsystematic. On top of that, our command of language may well be weak, inadequate, clumsy, and halting. And finally we often lack courage and boldness of speech – except perhaps when we are ignorant of what we are talking about. So it is hardly surprising that we find it hard to communicate.

Disappointingly, some of these very shortcomings can be discovered where one might least expect to find them: on the back covers of Charles Luk's and Robert Thurman's translations of the *Vimalakīrti-nirdeśa*. Both of these 'blurbs' – a very expressive and appropriate word – betray fundamental misunderstandings about Vimalakīrti's status as a layman.

The back cover of the American edition of Luk's translation tells us that the text is 'particularly applicable to Western Buddhist students because it expounds the practice that a layman may follow'. When I first saw this sentence, I could hardly believe my eyes. Is being able to teach the Dharma to such Arhants as Śāriputra and Mahā-Maudgalyāyana and such Bodhisattvas as Maitreya part of 'the practice that a layman may follow'? Is bringing thirty-two thousand lion-thrones from a distant Buddha-land and accommodating them all in one small house part of 'the practice that a layman may follow'? Vimalakīrti discourses about Wisdom and Compassion with Mañjuśrī, reveals other universes, emanates a golden Bodhisattva, and transports thousands of beings into the presence of the Buddha. Is all this part of 'the practice that a layman may follow'? One wonders what sort of layman the blurb writer had in mind.

And on the back cover of Thurman's translation we find something almost as bad. Here the blurb says, among other things, 'His [Vimalakīrti's] message is particularly appealing to our secular age, because he was a man of the world, not a monk or saint.' One would have thought that if Vimalakīrti's message appealed to our secular age, that would be a sure sign that it had been misunderstood.

There is so much confusion of thought in these two short sentences that it is hard to know where to begin to sort it out. The first claims that the *Vimalakīrti-nirdeśa* 'expounds the practice that a layman may follow', the second that Vimalakīrti 'was a man of the world'. The reasoning, such as it is, seems to be as follows. Vimalakīrti was a layman. Therefore Vimalakīrti 'was a man of the world'. Therefore Vimalakīrti's teaching expounds 'the practice a layman may follow'. Therefore Vimalakīrti's message 'is particularly appealing to our secular age'.

But Vimalakīrti was *not* a layman: that is the whole point. Vimalakīrti lived like a layman, *appeared* to be a layman, but that was only his skilful means. In reality he was an advanced Bodhisattva. As the text says: 'He wore the white clothes of a layman, yet lived impeccably like a religious devotee. He lived at home, but remained aloof from the realm of desire, the realm of pure matter, and the immaterial realm. He had a son, a wife, and female attendants, yet always maintained continence. He appeared to be surrounded by servants, yet lived in solitude.'

It is easy enough to see how the whole misunderstanding has arisen. The blurb writers simply did not reflect on the real meaning of the words they used. They did not realize that the terms 'layman' and 'man of the world' mean one thing when applied to Vimalakīrti, who was a layman only in a formal technical sense, but quite another when applied to the sort of real lay people who might buy and read an English translation of the text.

To say that Vimalakīrti's teaching 'expounds the practice a layman may follow' is to imply that the layperson who wishes to practise the spiritual life does not have to give anything up. He or she can just carry on living at home with their partner, children, job, car, dog, cat, television, and mortgage. The crux of the matter, the underlying mental confusion, is the view that you don't really have to change. According to this view, you can practise the sublimest teaching of the Mahāyāna without giving up anything, without changing in any way. You can practise it staying at home as an ordinary layman, a 'man of the world'. Why? Because Vimalakīrti was an ordinary layman, Vimalakīrti was 'a man of the world'....

But Vimalakīrti's own teaching to 'ordinary laymen' carries quite the opposite implication. As we have seen, he has created the opportunity to speak to a whole crowd of laymen by appearing to be ill as a skilful means, and thousands of people have come to enquire after his health. According to the text, the king himself is among the visitors, as well as government officials, lords, young men and women, townsfolk and country folk, aristocrats, and businessmen – a real cross-section of lay society. And Vimalakīrti's teaching to all these people is not that they should stay at home and carry on just as before. Instead, he strikes right at the heart of the matter, right at the one thing that we are most unwilling to give up: the physical body. Giving up the physical body means death; it means the loss of all the pleasures that we enjoy through the senses. Towards the end of chapter 2, Vimalakīrti declares:

> 'Friends, this body is so impermanent, fragile, unworthy of confidence, and feeble. It is so insubstantial, perishable, short-lived, painful, filled with diseases, and subject to changes. Thus, my friends, as this body is only a vessel of many sicknesses, wise men do not rely on it. This body is like a ball of foam, unable to bear any pressure. It is like a water bubble, not remaining very long. It is like a mirage, born from the appetites of the passions. It is like the trunk of

> the plantain tree, having no core. Alas! This body is like a machine, a nexus of bones and tendons. It is like a magical illusion, consisting of falsifications. It is like a dream, being an unreal vision. It is like a reflection, being the image of former actions. It is like an echo, being dependent on conditioning. It is like a cloud, being characterized by turbulence and dissolution. It is like a flash of lightning, being unstable, and decaying every moment. The body is ownerless, being the product of a variety of conditions.
>
> 'This body is inert, like the earth; selfless, like water; lifeless, like fire; impersonal, like the wind; and nonsubstantial, like space. This body is unreal, being a collocation of the four main elements. It is void, not existing as self or as self-possessed. It is inanimate, being like grass, trees, walls, clods of earth, and hallucinations. It is insensate, being driven like a windmill. It is filthy, being an agglomeration of pus and excrement. It is false, being fated to be broken and destroyed, in spite of being anointed and massaged. It is afflicted by the four hundred and four diseases. It is like an ancient well, constantly overwhelmed by old age. Its duration is never certain – certain only is its end in death. This body is a combination of aggregates, elements, and sense-media, which are comparable to murderers, poisonous snakes, and an empty town, respectively. Therefore, you should be revulsed by such a body. You should despair of it and should arouse your admiration for the body of the Tathāgata.'[31]

So much for the mortal, human body. Now for a different sort of body, the embodiment of the highest spiritual ideal:

> 'Friends, the body of a Tathāgata is the body of Dharma, born of gnosis. The body of a Tathāgata is born of the stores of merit and wisdom. It is born of morality, of meditation, of wisdom, of the liberations, and of the knowledge and vision of liberation. It is born of love, compassion, joy, and impartiality. It is born of charity, discipline, and self-control. It is born of the path of ten virtues. It is born of patience and gentleness. It is born of the roots of virtue planted by solid efforts. It is born of the concentrations, the liberations, the meditations, and the absorptions. It is born of learning, wisdom, and liberative technique. It is born of the thirty-seven aids to enlightenment. It is born of mental quiescence and transcendental analysis. It is born of the ten powers, the four fearlessnesses, and the eighteen special qualities. It is born of all the

> transcendences. It is born from sciences and superknowledges. It is born of the abandonment of all evil qualities, and of the collection of all good qualities. It is born of reality. It is born of conscious awareness.
>
> 'Friends, the body of a Tathāgata is born of innumerable good works. Toward such a body you should turn your aspirations, and, in order to eliminate the sicknesses of the passions of all living beings, you should conceive the spirit of unexcelled, perfect enlightenment.'[32]

Such, then, is the true nature of Vimalakīrti's advice to 'laymen'. It is not exactly an exhortation to go home and put your feet up. Vimalakīrti the layman cannot meaningfully be a model for members of the Sangha, either individually or collectively, for the simple reason that he is, we are told, a fully Enlightened Bodhisattva who simply appears as a householder as a skilful means. Before you can behave like Vimalakīrti, you have got to be a Buddha. His external life-style can only be a model inasmuch as it shows that you can pursue the spiritual path under a certain set of conditions. But commitment to that Path in principle must precede following it in that particular way. In other words, commitment must precede life-style. You don't imitate Vimalakīrti simply by living as a layman, because Vimalakīrti was not just anybody living as a layman. What made Vimalakīrti what he was was not his life-style, but his spiritual attainment – so to imitate him, you have to imitate his spiritual attainment.

According to the Pali scriptures the Buddha started off as an ordinary human being who gained Enlightenment by his own efforts. So we can follow in the Buddha's footsteps even though we may not do exactly the things the Buddha did. And to follow – or imitate – the Buddha means, first of all, gaining Enlightenment. But Vimalakīrti is presented to us as being a Buddha already. His human life represents not an effort to gain Enlightenment, but rather an approach by a Buddha to other human beings purely as a skilful means. Vimalakīrti may act in a certain way which appears to us as ethical, but he does not act in that way to attain Buddhahood, because he has already attained it. He is acting in that way as a skilful means. So if we want to imitate Vimalakīrti, we have to imitate the actions he performs as a skilful means; and we can't do that unless we have gained Buddhahood first.

Imitating Vimalakīrti, in short, means imitating Vimalakīrti. It doesn't mean imitating what Vimalakīrti does without being Vimalakīrti, without being a Buddha. In the strict Mahāyāna sense, skilful means is an expression of Enlightenment, not something that the ordinary person can engage in. What we *can* infer from the example of Vimalakīrti is that commitment to practice – effort in the direction of Enlightenment – is primary, and life-style is secondary. Being a monk or nun does not automatically guarantee you spiritual progress, and being a layperson need not be a handicap. This is not to say, of course, that life-style is unimportant; one's way of life should be both an expression of one's commitment to spiritual practice and a support to it.

This is not how the whole Buddhist tradition views this matter, of course. What is sometimes known as the 'monastic–lay split' crops up again and again in Buddhist history, with some traditions giving more 'status' to those who lead a 'monastic' life than to 'laymen' – regardless, sometimes, of who is the more faithful practitioner of the Dharma. In the Tibetan tradition, however, there are Dharma practitioners and teachers following different life-styles: some of them happen to be lay people, and others happen to be monks or nuns. For instance, Milarepa's teacher Marpa was a married householder, and his disciple Gampopa was a monk, while Milarepa himself was an itinerant yogi. In the Vajrayāna there is not the dichotomy between monk follower and lay follower that is found in the Hīnayāna and even to some extent in the Mahāyāna. Practising the teachings and achieving the fruits of that practice is not seen as dependent on following a particular life-style. Some of the most prominent Nyingmapa lamas of recent times have been married. The Gelugpas, on the other hand, are essentially monastic. In the Western Buddhist Order we also regard commitment to practice as primary and life-style as secondary. So we also do not emphasize a difference between monks and laity.

(3) The *Dhāraṇīs* or 'Magical Formulae

Now we come to the third aspect of the skilful means practised by the Bodhisattva. Traditionally, a *dhāraṇī* is a sort of protective mantra – or at least it is on its way to being a mantra. Historically speaking, mantras would appear to be a further evolution of *dhāraṇīs*. *Dhāraṇīs* are usually much longer – some go on for pages – and their conceptual content is often quite considerable. Mantras, by contrast, are almost always short, often have a minimum of conceptual content, and are usually connected with a particular Buddha or Bodhisattva in a way that a *dhāraṇī* is not. The *dhāraṇī* seems on the whole to have been used in a purely magical way, whereas a mantra is often repeated as an aid to concentration, and therefore becomes a part of meditation practice in a way that a *dhāraṇī* rarely does.

A *dhāraṇī* has some sort of magical power or potency; it brings about results. It is usually given to the Bodhisattva by a friendly deity, and it is supposed to protect him from any danger he may encounter in the course of his work. There is no reason why we should not take this traditional explanation quite literally. But more broadly, we may also see the *dhāraṇīs* as giving a touch of magic, a touch of the inconceivable, a hint of something beyond words, beyond thoughts. Inasmuch as 'spiritual experience' takes place within the dualistic subject–object framework, the *dhāraṇī* can even be said to give a touch of something beyond spiritual experience. And this touch of magic is indispensable to the Bodhisattva's practice of skilful means. This kind of skilful means is less accessible to us than the others; the use of *dhāraṇīs* as skilful means is a mysterious and subtle business, and one would really have to be a Bodhisattva to see how it works.

All the ways of practising skilful means we have explored are specific aspects of the Bodhisattva's interaction with other people. But the practice of skilful means is broader than this. Indeed, the whole of the Dharma is a skilful means, the greatest of all skilful means. And we can define the Dharma as whatever helps us to grow, whatever conduces to our spiritual development. But even the Dharma cannot be a skilful means in the abstract. You can't find it in a book. A skilful means is a skilful means only to the extent that it is practised, only to the extent that it is lived out.

So if we want the Buddha's discovery of the truth of things to be more widely known, we ourselves must become a skilful means. We must communicate our vision of what men and women can become, and make every effort to transform ourselves in the light of that vision. If we are generous and open in our dealings with people, if we speak to them kindly and affectionately, if we succeed in inspiring them, in sparking them off, and if we show that we ourselves are at least making an effort to evolve, we will be practising skilful means. And if we have some experience of the truth and reality of things, if we think clearly, if we express ourselves adequately, and if we are full of courage and self-confidence, we will be able to communicate our vision to others. Above all, our actions and our communication need a little touch of magic, a touch of the inconceivable, a touch of that which is beyond words. Then, and only then, we shall truly be able to be 'all things to all men'.

4

THE TRANSCENDENTAL CRITIQUE OF RELIGION

ONCE OUR BASIC NEEDS for food, clothing, shelter, and leisure have been met, what do we need more than anything else in life? What is our essential need as human beings? Surely it is freedom. The real meaning of human life is to develop our distinctively human characteristics: awareness, emotional positivity, responsibility for ourselves and others, and creativity. But we cannot develop, we cannot grow, unless we have space – both literally and metaphorically – to grow into. We need freedom: freedom from all that restricts us, both outside us and within us, freedom from our own conditioning, even freedom from our old self.

And what helps us to be free – apart from our own efforts – is, or at least is considered to be, religion. We have seen that in Buddhism the spiritual life is frequently described in terms of freedom, but Buddhism is not alone in this. The followers of other religions, at least the universal religions, would probably also say that their religion stands for the freedom of the individual. The Christian might quote from the New Testament the words: 'You shall know the truth, and the truth shall make you free.'[33]

But if we consider what it is that stops us from becoming free – apart from our own sloth and torpor, laziness, neglect, forgetfulness, and so on – we encounter a tremendous paradox. Strangely enough, religion, rather than helping us to become spiritually free, only too often helps to keep us enslaved, and even adds further shackles to our chains. To many people, the very idea that religion has anything to do with freedom sounds like an absurd contradiction in terms. Some people, and I must confess that I am among them, feel uncomfortable using – in a sense being obliged to use – the word 'religion' at all.

We find it so difficult to associate religion with freedom – we in the West, that is – not because of what religion is in principle, but rather because of its historical record. Take, for example, the record of Christianity over the last sixteen hundred years, since it was declared the official religion of the Roman Empire. It is fairly obvious that we cannot develop as individuals unless we are free at least to think for ourselves. But organized Christianity – certainly in the form of its major churches – has hardly ever allowed the individual that freedom. People in Christian countries have been obliged to think as the Church thought, to toe the theological line – or face the consequences. Even today, what the Church calls blasphemy is still a criminal offence in Britain.

Not only has organized Christianity refused to allow individuals to think for themselves. It has made them think in ways actually detrimental, actually inimical, to their own personal development. It has made them think of themselves as miserable sinners, as weak and powerless, made them think that being independent and taking the initiative is wrong, if not positively sinful.

So what went wrong? How is it that religion has become not a liberator but a jailer? The short answer is that religion has become an end in itself. The forms which religion takes – doctrines, rituals, institutions, rules – have all become ends in themselves. It has been forgotten that religion is a means to an end – that end being the individual's development from ignorance to Enlightenment, from mundane consciousness to transcendental consciousness.

What are we to do in this situation? We need to grow, we need to become free, and we need something to help us do so. If we agree to call that thing 'religion', how are we to make sure that religion does not become a means of enslaving or stultifying, even of crushing, the individual? We need something that will constantly remind us of the limitations of religion, something that will constantly remind us that religion is only a means to an end. In other words, we need a transcendental critique of religion. And in chapters 3 and 4 of the *Vimalakīrti-nirdeśa* we find such a critique. In Thurman's translation these chapters are entitled 'The Disciples' Reluctance to Visit Vimalakīrti' and 'The Reluctance of the Bodhisattvas'.

We have already learned that, out of his skilful means, out of his great Compassion, Vimalakīrti has fallen sick. Many people have come to visit him and enquire after his health, and he has taken the opportunity of teaching them the Dharma. At the beginning of chapter 3, we find Vimalakīrti at home, in his own room, lying on his bed. And as he lies there, a thought passes through his mind – or perhaps, as he is an advanced Bodhisattva, we should say that he allows a thought to pass through his mind. He thinks

> 'I am sick, lying on my bed in pain, yet the Tathāgata, the saint, the perfectly accomplished Buddha, does not consider me or take pity upon me, and sends no one to inquire after my illness.'

The Buddha, meanwhile, is in Āmrapālī's garden on the outskirts of the city of Vaiśālī teaching the great assembly of Arhants, Bodhisattvas, and others. And as he sits there teaching, the Buddha becomes aware of the thought passing through Vimalakīrti's mind. It's as though the two of them are playing a sort of game. After all, Vimalakīrti is not really sick in the ordinary sense, and presumably the Buddha knows that, but he seems quite happy to play his part in the game, quite willing to 'play ball'.

So what is his next move? Knowing the thought that is passing through Vimalakīrti's mind, the Buddha says: 'Śāriputra,' – in the Mahāyāna sūtras it always seems to be poor old Śāriputra who gets singled out – 'go to inquire after the illness of Vimalakīrti.' Or, as we would say, 'Please go and enquire after his health' – an interesting difference of idiom.

Śāriputra is one of the two leading disciples of the Buddha, the other being Mahā-Maudgalyāyana. He is an Arhant, so he has gained individual emancipation, he is liberated at least from the ordinary passions. But what does he say? He says 'I am reluctant to go', or, more literally, 'I am not very keen on going.' He does not actually refuse – after all, it is the Buddha who is asking him to go – but he would much rather not, and he explains why. One day, he says, he was sitting at the foot of a tree in the forest – as good monks were supposed to do in ancient India – absorbed in contemplation, when Vimalakīrti happened to pass by. 'That is not the way to absorb yourself in contemplation,' he told Śāriputra. And he proceeded to explain what absorption in contemplation really was. His explanation was so profound that Śāriputra was left dumbfounded, and quite unable to reply. This is why he is unwilling to go and ask Vimalakīrti about his illness. He has had some experience of Vimalakīrti before, and he is not very keen on encountering him again.

The Buddha tries again. He asks Mahā-Maudgalyāyana to go. But, strange to say, Mahā-Maudgalyāyana is also reluctant. It seems that he too has been rebuked by Vimalakīrti. One day, when he was teaching the Dharma to some householders, Vimalakīrti came along and told him how it should really be done – and Mahā-Maudgalyāyana was also left dumbfounded by his remarks.

In this way, the Buddha asks ten of the leading Arhant disciples to go. He asks Mahākāśyapa, Subhūti, Pūrṇa, Kātyāyana, Aniruddha, Upāli, Rāhula, even Ānanda. But, one and all, they are reluctant to go; they have all had some previous experience of dear old Vimalakīrti. He has exposed the spiritual shortcomings of them all. In doing so, he has exposed, in fact, as we shall see, the spiritual shortcomings of the Hīnayāna when its teachings are taken literally, taken as ends in themselves.

So the Buddha turns to the Bodhisattvas who are also in the great assembly. (One gets the impression that he is rather enjoying this little game.) He asks Maitreya to go and enquire about Vimalakīrti's illness. Maitreya is of course the future Buddha, who at present resides in the Tuṣita *devaloka*, the 'contented' heaven, waiting for the time when he will be reborn on earth for his last life, in which he will himself gain supreme perfect Enlightenment as a Buddha. But even he, even Maitreya, would rather not go. He too has already encountered Vimalakīrti.

One day, he says, while he was speaking with the gods of the Tuṣita heaven, Vimalakīrti turned up, and said

> 'Maitreya, the Buddha has prophesied that after one more birth you will attain supreme perfect Enlightenment. But what is the nature of that birth? Is it past, present, or future?'

And he went on to show, with great dialectical skill, that it could not be any of these. He showed that the very notion of birth – and also the notion of birthlessness – is self-contradictory. He showed that in reality there is no such thing as the attainment of Enlightenment – in fact, no such thing as Enlightenment at all. He even showed that there is no such thing as Maitreya, no such thing as a future Buddha. Maitreya was rendered speechless. He too is therefore reluctant to go to Vimalakīrti and enquire about his illness.

The Buddha next asks Prabhāvyūha; but Prabhāvyūha has had a similar experience. One day he just happened to meet Vimalakīrti, who asked him where he was coming from – an innocent enough question.

Prabhāvyūha replied that he was coming from the *bodhimaṇḍa*, the 'place of Enlightenment'. In other words, he was coming from Bodh-gaya, where the Buddha gained supreme perfect Enlightenment, and in particular from the *vajrāsana*, the diamond throne, the place where the Buddha sat under the Bodhi tree. That was where he was coming from, he said. Vimalakīrti thereupon explained to him at some length that the *bodhimaṇḍa* is not really a place at all but a state of mind, something from which there is no question of a Bodhisattva coming, because he is in it all the time. Everything a Bodhisattva does is an expression of it. Not unnaturally, Prabhāvyūha too was rendered speechless, and thus he also is reluctant to visit Vimalakīrti. He does not want another dose of the same medicine.

The Buddha asks two more of the great Bodhisattvas – Jagatımdhara and Sudatta – to go, but for similar reasons they too are reluctant. In the end the Buddha asks Mañjuśrī, the Bodhisattva of Wisdom – but that is another story, and what happens next we will see in the next chapter. The point here is that Vimalakīrti has exposed the spiritual shortcomings of Maitreya and the other Bodhisattvas. He has, in other words, exposed the spiritual shortcomings of the Mahāyāna taken literally, taken as an end in itself.

It is fairly obvious what Vimalakīrti represents here, but not so easy to put it into words. We could say that Vimalakīrti represents Truth or Reality itself devoid of all concepts. That will do provided we don't take it too literally, provided we don't let it roll off the tongue too glibly. We could say that Vimalakīrti represents the actual Enlightenment experience. For what happens when our partial spiritual experiences are brought into contact with Truth or Reality? What happens when the means to Enlightenment – our rituals, our doctrines, our institutions, our rules – are brought into contact with the Enlightenment experience?

What happens is that their limitations are revealed. And this can be a very painful and traumatic experience indeed – painful and traumatic, that is, for those who identify themselves with their own partial spiritual experiences, and derive their emotional security from that identification. Vimalakīrti is like a high-voltage current of electricity. You touch him at your peril – except that you don't touch him; he comes along and touches you. In traditional terms, Vimalakīrti is like a great vajra, a great thunderbolt or diamond. He is powerful, he is incisive, and at the same time he is brilliant and scintillating. He bursts through all your defences, all your limitations. He destroys what you are so that you are free to become what you can be.

Vimalakīrti's effect on people reminds me of the main character in a film I saw some years ago: Pasolini's *Theorem*. In this film, in a very brief space of time, this one person has a tremendous impact on the lives of those who encounter him. He is a young salesman who spends the weekend with a middle-class Italian family. (He has some business with the father of the family, who is the head of an industrial concern.) The family consists of father, mother, grown-up son, grown-up daughter, and not-so-young maidservant, and in the course of the weekend the young man manages to have affairs with all of them. The rest of the film shows the dramatic results of their contact with him. The mother becomes a nymphomaniac. The daughter has a nervous breakdown; we see her being taken away in an ambulance to a mental hospital. The son, an artist, destroys all his paintings. The maidservant becomes a nun and works miracles. In the last scene the father is seen walking through a crowded railway station slowly taking off his clothes. The critics, I remember, had a field day discussing the meaning of this film, especially what the young man represented. Some said that he was a sort of Christ figure, others that he symbolized reality – and some thought he was just being himself.

In these two chapters of the *Vimalakīrti-nirdeśa*, the irruption of Vimalakīrti into the lives of the disciples and the Bodhisattvas happens on a much higher level, and has a much more positive effect – but it is still devastating. The impact of reality in any form has a shattering effect on anyone's life. Each of the disciples and Bodhisattvas concerned is left dumbfounded. Thurman comments: 'He' – the disciple or the Bodhisattva – 'is overwhelmed and speechless, yet intuitively recognizes the rightness of Vimalakīrti's statements. He can neither accept them and put them into practice nor reject them outright.'[34]

This is perhaps something that we too may experience on our own level of development. When our *kalyāna mitra*, our 'good friend', points out something about our own character that we have not noticed before, or something about the Dharma that is new to us, to begin with we may feel simply stunned. We have to recognize the truth of what is being said but, initially at least, we are quite unable to do anything about it. It takes time to adjust to new knowledge and put it into practice.

So it is not surprising that the disciples and the Bodhisattvas are 'no very keen' on going to meet Vimalakīrti. It is not surprising that the partial experience should be reluctant to encounter the total experience, that the means to Enlightenment should be reluctant to encounter Enlightenment itself. The experience is too painful, too traumatic. But although it may be painful, or even traumatic, it is highly positive. The purpose of Vimalakīrti's strictures is not to humiliate the disciples and the Bodhisattvas. He is not just 'putting them down'. His purpose is to help them to move on from their present partial experience, their present relatively limited outlook. (It is only *relatively* limited because they are, after all, Arhants and Bodhisattvas.)

We also need to bear in mind that Vimalakīrti's behaviour here exemplifies the skilful means of an advanced Bodhisattva. When we ourselves feel the need to criticize someone's behaviour, we need to make sure that we are doing so from a positive basis. We should certainly be careful not to upset people for the sake of it. At the same time, we should not hold back from speaking the truth simply because people may find it upsetting. If you can put your point effectively in a gentle way, that is clearly best. But very often a point does not get across to people unless it has some edge. They may be so closed to any views other than their own that a dignified, objective, and emotionally neutral statement of your point of view has little effect, in which case you may have to express yourself more trenchantly. And unfortunately it is not always possible to make a point without making a personal criticism of someone. If their views stem directly from their character, and you are criticizing those views, you can hardly help criticizing their character too. The purpose of criticism is to help someone grow and develop. Therefore, the rule of thumb is to upset people as little as possible, while still saying what you feel must be said.

In the same way, the purpose of the transcendental critique of religion is not to destroy religion, but rather to restore it to its true function, which is to be a means to an end, a means to the spiritual development of the individual. All that is destroyed is religion as an end in itself. The transcendental critique of religion is therefore essential to the very existence of religion. It must accompany it all the time. It is important to understand this; it's important to understand it in detail. So let us look a little more closely at the encounters of some of the Buddha's disciples, Pūrṇa, Upāli, Rāhula, and Ānanda, and the Bodhisattva Jagatīṁdhara, with Vimalakīrti.

First, the disciple Pūrṇa. Pūrṇa was teaching the Hīnayāna doctrine to some young monks in the forest when Vimalakīrti came along. And Vimalakīrti said that Pūrṇa was teaching the monks wrongly, because they were capable of following the Mahāyāna, which was a higher teaching. Now, Vimalakīrti was not criticizing Pūrṇa simply for teaching the Hīnayāna instead of the Mahāyāna. After all, as we have seen, he was quite capable of exposing the limitations of the Mahāyāna too, considered as an end in itself. He was criticizing Pūrṇa for teaching the Dharma mechanically, without looking to see what the spiritual needs of the young monks really were.

He said

> 'Reverend Pūrṇa, first concentrate yourself, regard the minds of these young bhikṣus, and then teach them the Dharma! Do not put rotten food into a jeweled bowl! First understand the inclination of these monks, and do not confuse priceless sapphires with glass beads!
>
> 'Reverend Pūrṇa, without examining the spiritual faculties of living beings, do not presume upon the one-sidedness of their faculties; do not wound those who are without wounds; do not impose a narrow path upon those who aspire to a great path; do not try to pour the great ocean into the hoof-print of an ox; do not try to put Mount Sumeru into a grain of mustard; do not confuse the brilliance of the sun with the light of a glowworm; and do not expose those who admire the roar of a lion to the howl of a jackal!'[35]

As a result of listening to Vimalakīrti's critique, Pūrṇa realized:

> 'The disciples, who do not know the thoughts or the inclinations of others, are not able to teach the Dharma to anyone.'

This is a pretty strong statement. Vimalakīrti is criticizing Pūrṇa for not being in real communication with the people he is teaching. Pūrṇa seems to have a fixed idea about the Dharma, to think that it consists in *this* particular teaching and *that* particular conceptual formulation; and this is what he conveys to the people he teaches, regardless of whether or not it will actually help them to develop.

Some Eastern Buddhist teachers tend to do this when they come to the West. They have learned about the Dharma in the East and they think that all they have to do is repeat it in the West. But to communicate the Dharma effectively, you need to be aware of the spiritual needs of the people you are teaching – and this takes time. Vimalakīrti is not criticizing Pūrṇa for teaching the Dharma; he is criticizing him for teaching it in the wrong way, for regarding the teaching of the Dharma as an end in itself.

I found myself teaching the Dharma 'in the wrong way' in India some years ago. I was asked to lecture regularly on full moon days at a certain Buddhist hall in Calcutta. A lot of people, in fact hundreds of people, mostly Bengali Buddhists, used to come, but I soon realized that they had not come to listen to the Dharma. They saw the occasion as a social gathering, and there would always be quite a lot of noise, shouting and talking, going on. What they actually wanted was a monk just talking quietly away in the corner, lending a faint air of religiosity to the proceedings. My suspicions were confirmed when I eventually complained to the head monk about the behaviour of the audience (although they weren't really an *audience* because they weren't listening). He said 'It doesn't matter if nobody can hear what you're saying; we just want you to lecture on the Dharma.' A lecture on the Dharma had become part of the social ritual. Someone had to be seen to be giving it, but it didn't matter whether or not anybody could hear or understand what was being said. The whole thing had become quite meaningless. So I had actually been asked to teach the Dharma 'in the wrong way'. This is an example – rather an extreme one – of the sort of thing that Vimalakīrti is getting at.

Now for Upāli's encounter with Vimalakīrti. Among all the Buddha's disciples, Upāli was the great expert in the *Vinaya* or monastic law, and it was because of this expertise that one day he was approached by two monks. They had committed some offence against the monastic rule, and, ashamed to appear before the Buddha, they went instead to Upāli and asked him to remove their anxieties by accepting their confession and witnessing their promise not to commit the offence again – that being the regular monastic procedure. Upāli agreed, and into the bargain gave them what the text calls a 'religious discourse'.

At this point Vimalakīrti came along and said that Upāli was only making matters worse. He said

> 'Reverend Upāli, do not aggravate further the sins of these two monks. Without perplexing them, relieve their remorse. Reverend Upāli, sin is not to be apprehended within, or without, or between the two. Why? The Buddha has said, "Living beings are afflicted by the passions of thought, and they are purified by the purification of thought."'[36]

He went on to say quite a lot more of a metaphysical nature, but this passage is enough for our present purpose. What is Vimalakīrti getting at? Why does he say that Upāli is only making matters worse? What does he mean by saying that there is no such thing as sin? Let us look at the situation. The two monks have committed an offence – that is, they have broken a rule. But why was the rule laid down in the first place? It was laid down to help the individual – in this case the individual monk – to grow spiritually. Having broken the rule, the two monks have put an obstacle in the way of their spiritual development. They have perhaps even regressed. So Upāli should not be concerned simply with the fact that they have broken the rule; that would be to treat the rule as an end in itself. His main concern, Vimalakīrti is implying, should be to get them back on the right path.

Belief in 'sin' is nothing but a stumbling block which arises out of treating rules as ends in themselves. When we break them, 'sin' comes into existence, and we waste time worrying about how to get rid of it instead of getting on with the task of our individual development. This is of course an essentially Christian predicament. If you believe in God, and the laws or commandments he is said to have laid down, what happens if you break one of those rules? 'Sin' comes into existence, and you feel guilt and fear of punishment. And when this happens, you need someone to save you from the consequences of your sin: a saviour. All this is what is known as 'religion' in the West. In fact, the situation is even more complicated, because sin came into existence before we were even born, when Adam and Eve disobeyed God and ate of the tree of the knowledge of good and evil. According to the Christian tradition, sin is our inheritance; we are born into sin. This is the predicament of the Christian, as well as that of the ex-Christian who is not aware that past indoctrination is still having an effect. It is to avoid such a predicament that we need to be aware of the danger of regarding rules as ends in themselves. This is why Vimalakīrti takes Upāli so firmly to task.

Vimalakīrti says that there is no such thing as sin. He says

> 'Sin is not to be apprehended within, or without, or between the two.'

In other words, sin is a mere concept, a mere word. Consider the effect of doing something unskilful. It will in most cases have affected someone else, and it is important that one should regret that. But this is only part of it. The action will also have had the effect of hindering one's own spiritual progress. If you have something of which to repent, your urge to develop has weakened, at least to some degree, and it needs to be revitalized. The two things – repentance for what you have done and renewal of your inspiration – are closely interlinked.

Vimalakīrti is simply making the point that your concern should go beyond your failures. Yes, you do have to repent unskilful acts, you have to resolve to do better, you have to experience remorse. But you must also make sure that you revive your original inspiration; because it was due to the flagging of that inspiration that you committed the unskilful action in the first place. So you have to deal with the unskilful action itself – and possibly with its consequences – but within the context of reviving your inspiration. The two are not alternatives; you really need to do both. In fact, one might say that you can genuinely repent only if there is a genuine revival of your inspiration.

So the first thing you have to do is try to understand what you have done. Then you cultivate a sense of regret that you have done it, especially if it has involved injury to another person. Thirdly, you resolve not to do that particular thing again. And fourthly, you take steps to ensure that in future you do what is right. 'Sin' does not come into it at all. That's why Vimalakīrti quotes the Buddha as saying:

> 'Living beings are afflicted by the passions of thought, and they are purified by the purification of thought.'

As to the steps you take to modify your behaviour in future, here you must tread carefully. It is probably not helpful, for example, to think in terms of penances. It is important to remember that you are not punishing yourself. 'Discipline' is probably a better word to use in a Buddhist context. For example, suppose you became aware that your behaviour was unskilful with regard to food – that you were greedy – and you therefore decided to limit your intake of food. That would be an attempt to retrain yourself, to modify your behaviour based on your understanding. It would not be a punishment for eating too much.

The term penance, as ordinarily used, seems to mean something halfway between a punishment and a discipline. A penance is intended to 'pay for', 'make up for', what one has done. For example, a Catholic may be given the penance of, say, reciting ten 'Hail Marys' – quite a mild penance for some small sin – and it is presumably intended to inspire the penitent with thoughts of the Virgin Mary so that they don't commit that sin again. But if it is taken as a sort of spiritual bookkeeping, it probably doesn't contribute all that much to spiritual development. Often people know in advance what sort of penance they will get if they commit a particular sin; they know that they will do the penance and then they will be 'quits'. You then get a cycle of unskilful action – penance – unskilful action – penance – and so on. In the end you hardly remember which came first. You can even end up thinking in terms of having permission to do something unskilful because you have done the penance, in which case there will be no real modification of your behaviour or mental attitude. Penance has spiritual value only when it is seen not as a sort of punishment but as a discipline, intelligently imposed upon oneself in order to check certain unskilful attitudes and develop more skilful ones.

One has to be careful not to put oneself through a kind of aversion therapy, in which one instils an unconscious reaction or revulsion against a particular course of action. Clearly this sort of counter-conditioning can have no spiritual value, and probably no ethical value either. It results in 'ethical' behaviour through the most basic motivation: fear of pain if one does otherwise. One must guard against conditioning oneself in a particular way without properly understanding what is happening and without genuinely changing one's attitude.

Next we come to Vimalakīrti's encounter with Rāhula. Rāhula was, of course, the Buddha's son, and he had become his grandfather's heir after his father had left home and gone forth. So in going forth himself, Rāhula renounced not only the world, but also the throne. And when a number of Licchavi youths asked him why he had renounced the kingdom, he outlined for them the benefits and virtues of renouncing the world. But as he was getting into his stride, Vimalakīrti came along and said that Rāhula was explaining the matter all wrong. He said

> 'Renunciation is itself the very absence of virtues and benefits. Reverend Rāhula, one may speak of benefits and virtues in regard to compounded things, but renunciation is uncompounded, and there can be no question of benefits and virtues in regard to the uncompounded.'[37]

Renunciation – leaving the world – is essentially a spiritual activity. It is not a matter of *gaining* – even gaining benefits and virtues – but of growing. However, the young men still do not understand. They say

> 'We have heard the Tathāgata [the Buddha] declare that one should not renounce the world without the permission of one's parents.'

They are still thinking in formal terms: in terms of a formal leaving of the world, in terms of becoming a monk in a literal or technical sense. Vimalakīrti returns to his point more emphatically than ever. He says

> 'Young men, you should cultivate yourselves intensively to conceive the spirit of unexcelled, perfect enlightenment. That in itself will be your renunciation and high ordination!'

Renunciation consists in the development of the Bodhicitta, in Going for Refuge to the Three Jewels. 'Leaving the world' and 'becoming a monk' are not ends in themselves. Vimalakīrti is not saying that these forms of renunciation are unnecessary. He is saying that the outer action is of value only to the extent that it is the expression of an inner attitude. You are not a monk simply because you are wearing a yellow robe.

Now we come to the story of Ānanda's meeting with Vimalakīrti. Ānanda was the Buddha's personal attendant and companion for the last twenty years of the Buddha's life. Naturally he was in close contact with the Buddha, and sometimes we get the impression that he was quite attached to him as a person. One day, it seems, the Buddha was unwell and needed some milk to help him recover. So Ānanda took his begging-bowl and went to the mansion of a great brahmin family to beg for some. Vimalakīrti turned up and asked Ānanda what he was doing there so early in the morning, and Ānanda said

> 'The body of the Lord manifests some indisposition, and he needs some milk. Therefore, I have come to fetch some.'[38]

Vimalakīrti then proceeded to scold Ānanda for saying such a thing:

> 'Reverend Ānanda, the Tathāgatas have the body of the Dharma – not a body that is sustained by material food. The Tathāgatas have a transcendental body that has transcended all mundane qualities.... Reverend Ānanda, to believe there can be illness in such a body is irrational and unseemly!'

The gist of Vimalakīrti's reply is that the Buddha should not be identified with his physical body, but with the *dharmakāya*, the Body of Truth, the Body of Reality. The physical body – even that of the Buddha – is not an end in itself, but a means to Enlightenment. When you have seen the physical body of the Buddha, you should not think you have seen the Buddha himself. The Buddha is essentially the Enlightened mind.

Hearing this, Ānanda felt ashamed that he had misunderstood the Dharma in this way. But a voice from the sky spoke, telling Ānanda not to be ashamed. After all, the Buddha does in a sense have a body, at least for a while. The voice said

> 'Since the Buddha has appeared during the time of the five corruptions, he disciplines human beings by acting lowly and humble.'

The suggestion is that the Buddha's illness, like that of Vimalakīrti, is skilful means; so Ānanda should go and get the milk.

The Bodhisattva Jagatīṁdhara's encounter with Vimalakīrti happened as he was receiving an unexpected and extraordinary visit at home one day: a visit from Māra, the evil one.[39] Māra did not come as Māra, of course – Māra never does! He came disguised as Indra, the king of the gods, and accompanied by twelve thousand heavenly maidens, all singing and playing music. What a scene they must have presented: the glorious figure of the king of the gods – as he seemed to be – in a blaze of light, decked with jewels; the twelve thousand heavenly maidens, no doubt looking very elegant in all sorts of silken drapery, with their hair floating down their backs; and all of them singing and playing wonderful music. (Imagine perhaps a highly trained choir of twelve thousand singing Monteverdi's 'Vespers'.) Then Māra, as Indra, saluted Jagatīṁdhara very meekly and humbly, even going to the extreme of touching the Bodhisattva's feet with his head, before standing respectfully to one side.

Jagatīṁdhara was completely taken in by this – as one usually is by Māra's disguises. He rose to the occasion and delivered a little sermon – I think we can call it that – suitable for a god: a sermon on impermanence. Māra appeared to be deeply moved and, to show gratitude, asked Jagatīṁdhara to accept the twelve thousand divine maidens as his servants. But Jagatīṁdhara was not a complete fool. He declined the offer, saying that heavenly maidens were not suitable servants for someone like himself who had taken up the spiritual life.

At this point Vimalakīrti entered on the scene and exposed what was going on. He said to Jagatīṁdhara:

> 'Noble son, do not think that this is Indra! This is not Indra but the evil Māra, who has come to ridicule you.'[40]

And to Māra he said that since Jagatīṁdhara was unable to accept the divine maidens, he, Vimalakīrti, would give them a home.

Even the disciples and Bodhisattvas were reluctant to meet Vimalakīrti, so you can guess how Māra felt. He was absolutely terrified. He tried to make a quick getaway, but it was no use. In the end he had to hand over all twelve thousand heavenly maidens – who were of course really Māra's daughters in disguise. And Vimalakīrti set about teaching the heavenly maidens to practise the Dharma. In the end he taught them to develop the Bodhicitta, the will to supreme Enlightenment for the benefit of all beings. Even that is not the end of the story. Māra later tried to get his daughters back, but they returned to him inspired by the Dharma and ready to inspire others.

So what does all this mean? Māra's daughters, the heavenly maidens, represent the emotions, the passions, in their relatively crude and unrefined forms. Obviously one who has taken up the spiritual life should not succumb to them, but should have them well under control. This stage of development is represented by Jagatīṁdhara, whose name, significantly perhaps, means 'Ruler of the World'.

But control, conscious control, is not the last word in the spiritual life. Rejection is not enough. Asceticism is not an end in itself. After all, the emotions have to be converted; they have to be transformed; they have to contribute their energies to the spiritual life. It is this stage that is represented by Vimalakīrti.

According to Thurman there is a definitely Tantric element in the *Vimalakīrti-nirdeśa*, especially in this passage. This may well be so, but we should be careful not to misunderstand this possibility. We need to avoid falling into the trap of thinking that we are accepting Māra's daughters as Vimalakīrti did when we are really only succumbing to them like an ordinary person. The stage represented by Jagatīṁdhara is one that most of us will be in for a very long time – assuming we can reach it, that is. But in the long run, it is not an end in itself; it is only a means to an end.

Having taken a closer look at the encounters of some of the disciples and Bodhisattvas with Vimalakīrti, we should now be quite clear about the main point. As Vimalakīrti's 'transcendental critique' serves to remind us, the Hīnayāna is a means to an end. The Mahāyāna is a means to an end. Buddhism is a means to an end. Religion is a means to an end. And that end is the spiritual development of the individual.

This critique has always been part of Buddhism. The Buddha said 'I teach the Dharma under the figure of a raft.'[41] In other words, just as a raft is useful for getting you across the water, but you wouldn't carry it with you once you had reached dry land, so the Buddha's teaching is useful for carrying us across the waters of saṁsāra, but we will have no need for it when we have reached the other shore of Enlightenment. This sort of emphasis is particularly strong in the Mahāyāna, and strongest of all, perhaps, in Zen. You get Japanese and Chinese pictures of the Sixth Patriarch tearing up the *Diamond Sūtra*. There is the story of the travelling monk who needed fuel because he was cold, and chopped up the wooden Buddha images in the temple at which he was staying. And there is the master who famously said to his disciple 'If you meet the Buddha on the road, kill him!'

These are all rather extreme, rather bizarre ways of underlining the same message: that Buddhism is only a means to an end. It is because Buddhism has always been aware of the difference between means and ends that down the centuries it has remained spiritually alive. For the same reason, it has not on the whole been dogmatic or intolerant. It has never persecuted the followers of other religions, and the followers of one form of Buddhism have rarely persecuted the followers of another.

Other religions, it must frankly be said, are not really on a par with Buddhism in this respect. They do not always help the individual to become free. They do not really see themselves as a means to an end in the way that Buddhism does. The theistic religions are especially hampered in this respect. They have no critique of religion, whether transcendental or otherwise; they have no self-critique. It is therefore necessary that we apply the Buddhist critique to them, that we get Vimalakīrti to come along. And when we do this, we find only too often that other religions are not in fact means to the development of the individual at all. The critique perforce turns into a criticism.

Some people think that one should not criticize religions other than one's own, or even that one should not criticize religion at all. But such criticism is essential in revealing obstacles to one's development as an individual. It is only by means of a critique that we can ensure that the means to the development of the individual remains a means and does not harden into an end in itself.

We should therefore apply this critique, even this criticism, to everything that presents itself to us as religion. We should apply it to Christianity, apply it to Buddhism, apply it to the Hīnayāna, apply it to the Mahāyāna, apply it to the Vajrayāna. It is perhaps impressive that the *Vimalakīrti-nirdeśa*, a Mahāyāna text, shows up the imperfections of Bodhisattvas. This does not happen in any of the other well-known Mahāyāna sūtras; perhaps it is one of the distinctive functions of the *Vimalakīrti-nirdeśa* to reveal the Bodhisattvas' shortcomings. Of course, the Bodhisattvas whose behaviour Vimalakīrti criticizes are not apparently archetypal Bodhisattvas; perhaps they are novice Bodhisattvas. And, as we shall see, Mañjuśrī, *the* archetypal Bodhisattva, is shown as being almost perfect.

We need, of course, to make sure that we apply our critique appropriately; sometimes it is more appropriate to express appreciation. A guiding principle might be to apply the critique first and foremost to oneself. If we all applied this transcendental critique to our own spiritual practice, there would hardly be any need for a transcendental critique of religion in general, or of our own religion in particular. We must be careful not to knock away the very ladder by which we are climbing – not, at least, until we are ready to do without it. We need to apply the critique to whatever practices we undertake – whether it is meditation or devotional practice, reading books or attending lectures, living in a community or working in a Right Livelihood business. We need to stay alive to the crucial question: is it helping me to develop? We should never allow any of these things to become ends in themselves; they are all means to an end. If we can remember this, we ourselves will be living embodiments of the reality of religion, and at the same time living embodiments of the transcendental critique of religion. Religion will then help us to become free. And then perhaps we will have at least a foretaste of the inconceivable emancipation.

5

History Versus Myth in Humanity's Quest for Meaning

In 1956, the year in which the Buddhist world celebrated the two-thousand-five-hundredth anniversary of the Buddha's Enlightenment, I found myself in New Delhi at the invitation of the Indian government, along with other 'prominent Buddhists from the border areas', as the government was pleased to style us. I suppose they had in mind a picture of aboriginal Buddhists turning up from the jungles of Assam and West Bengal – and actually we did look a very motley bunch, in robes of all shades of red and orange and yellow.

Of all the celebrations and speeches and events that went on, the most interesting from my point of view was an exhibition of Asian Buddhist art. At that time it was probably one of the biggest such exhibitions ever mounted anywhere in the world, and all the different Buddhist countries – Japan, Cambodia, Thailand, Bhutan, Tibet, and so on – had their own sections. After the Indian section, which was vast, the biggest and perhaps the most important collection was that organized by the People's Republic of China. (This was still in the palmy days of Indo-Chinese friendship, before the 1962 border war.)

Some of the Chinese exhibits were magnificent – I had never seen anything like them. And I remember one especially: a full scale copy of an ancient mural painting which occupied the whole of one wall. It dated, as far as I remember, from the T'ang Dynasty, or perhaps even earlier, and it depicted a number of figures, all more or less life-size. But there were two of these figures, occupying the centre of the picture, that particularly stood out. To the left, under a jewelled canopy, a beautiful young man was seated on a magnificent lotus-throne. He was clad in all manner of silks and jewels, and surrounded by standing yellow-robed figures. From the position of his hands and fingers – his *mudra* – he seemed to be saying something to the other main figure, who was seated to the right within a sort of curtained pavilion. This was a very old man. His face was covered with tiny wrinkles and he had a long, white, rather wispy beard. He wore a blue-grey robe, the traditional robe of the Chinese scholar – though this was, as we shall see, artistic licence – and he was surrounded by more standing figures in white robes. From the position of his hands and fingers he seemed to be replying to the young man. The two figures were, of course, Mañjuśrī, the Bodhisattva of Wisdom, on the left, and Vimalakīrti, the wise elder of Vaiśālī, on the right. The painting illustrates the famous meeting between them which is described at the beginning of chapter 5 of the *Vimalakīrti-nirdeśa*: 'The Consolation of the Invalid'.

As we saw in the last chapter, all the Arhants and Bodhisattvas present in the Buddha's assembly were reluctant to go to enquire after Vimalakīrti's health. This was because each and every one of them had had a painful, perhaps even rather embarrassing, encounter with Vimalakīrti which had exposed the limitations of their particular approach to the Dharma. We will take up the story at the beginning of chapter 5, at which point Mañjuśrī has just agreed to visit the invalid. He is fully aware of the difficulties and dangers of the undertaking. He knows that if you come into contact with such a powerful current of spiritual electricity as Vimalakīrti, you may get a shock. But he says:

> 'Although he cannot be withstood by someone of my feeble defences, still, sustained by the grace of the Buddha, I will go to him and will converse with him as well as I can.'[42]

The word translated here as 'grace' is the Sanskrit word *adhiṣṭhāna*, which certainly does not mean 'grace' in the Christian sense. 'Grace' here is the non-dualistic influence of the Buddha's transcendental experience of Enlightenment as that influence appears within the framework of the dualism of subject and object. Because in reality there is no such dualistic split, this influence cannot really be said to have an external source, but it *appears* to have one.

You could see *adhiṣṭhāna* as a powerful influence emanating from a powerful spiritual source, an influence which can have a radically transforming effect on you if you open yourself up to it. But it is not automatic – which is why 'grace' is not really an adequate translation. It is not exactly that you have to earn it, but it certainly is related to your capacity to receive it. Even on an ordinary level, if you experience goodwill coming from another person, that will have an effect on you. Your state of consciousness will be altered to some degree, and you will respond on that basis. In the same way on a higher level, if you can experience goodwill coming from a person who has some spiritual realization, even some insight into the nature of reality, presumably that will have an even greater effect on you. In fact, *adhiṣṭhāna* is flowing from the Buddhas and Bodhisattvas all the time, just as light and heat are constantly radiating from the sun. And you will be benefited by it to the extent that you are receptive to it.

In Tibetan, *adhiṣṭhāna* is translated as *chin lab*, which literally means 'power-wave'. *Chin* also has connotations of 'majesty' and 'splendour'. We tend to understand the word 'power' in a purely secular sense, but the power of the transcendental is more like power in the sense of love: a powerful expression of mettā. Perhaps one could speak of a 'love-wave', or even a 'blessing' with a great deal of strength behind it.

Adhiṣṭhāna is something which seems to come from above rather than arising from below; it is something which is 'given' to one. It is like artistic inspiration. Usually inspiration is spoken of coming up from the depths. But sometimes it seems to come down from some higher power: after hearing the first performance of his oratorio 'The Creation', Haydn is said to have murmured: 'It came from above.' So *adhiṣṭhāna* is perhaps analogous to the artist's invocation of the Muses, where one addresses oneself to higher powers and asks for their blessing.

This raises the question of the nature of effort in the spiritual life. We need, it seems, to make the effort to be receptive, but this may sound like a contradiction in terms. Is it possible to invoke the Muses so vigorously that you can't hear them singing? Take the example of playing in an orchestra: you are making a tremendous effort, but at the same time you are being receptive. Are the two things really so antithetical? Do you have to stop doing everything in order to be receptive? Or take the art of writing: you can be making a very intense effort, but at the same time you do feel receptive; something is flowing into you.

The problem seems to be that we make the wrong kind of effort. This happens when you try to appropriate a higher experience as something to be incorporated into your existing being, when what you should be doing is incorporating your existing being into the experience in such a way that your existing being is transformed. This effort, which is really just wilful exertion, is an attempt to retain the experience within the existing structure of your being, without allowing it to change you. Until Enlightenment is attained, there will always be a conflict between appropriating and experiencing, between incorporating and surrendering. It is no good thinking that all effort is wilful effort, and therefore to be avoided. The solution to the problem of wilfulness is not simply to take things easy.

It may be that the effort you make is not distributed over a broad enough spectrum of interests, so that your spiritual life becomes rather one-sided, and you lose your motivation. If you are working in a Right Livelihood business, you may need to make an effort, even a great effort, to apply yourself to the work; but at the same time you need to make effort in meditation, in spiritual friendships, and so on. It is not that you have been placing too much stress on effort, but that the effort is not distributed sufficiently widely. There are two ways of solving this problem. You can either make some provision, in the course of every day or over a week or a month, for all your requirements or interests to be met; or else you can spend a few weeks, even a few months, concentrating on one, then a few weeks or months concentrating on another, and so on. Either way, over the period of, say, a year, all your requirements would be met.

However, Mañjuśrī does not have any such problems when he makes the effort to visit Vimalakīrti on his sick-bed, because he is 'sustained by the grace of the Buddha'. What Mañjuśrī means by *adhiṣṭhāna* is that he is not going to see Vimalakīrti under his own steam, as it were. He is not going to embark on the visit with any fixed idea; he is going to deal with the situation spontaneously – which means that he is not even going with a fixed idea of 'acting spontaneously'.

When Mañjuśrī says he will go and see Vimalakīrti, everybody in the assembly – except, of course, the Buddha, who just sits there smiling through it all – gets tremendously excited. They think that if these two come together there will be a wonderful discussion, a real clash as between two cymbals, out of which something truly profound and illuminating will emerge.

So eight thousand – a quarter – of the Bodhisattvas and five hundred – one-sixteenth – of the Arhants decide to accompany Mañjuśrī on his visit. (No doubt these numbers have some significance.) Many hundreds of thousands of gods and goddesses also decide to go, so a great retinue accompanies Mañjuśrī on his journey to the city of Vaiśālī. Fully aware of their approach, Vimalakīrti exercises his magical power and makes everything around him disappear. The house itself, all his attendants, all the furniture, the seats, the couches – everything vanishes. All that can be seen is old Vimalakīrti himself, lying on his couch, suspended in mid-air.

At this point Mañjuśrī arrives. It would not be quite accurate to say that he enters, because there is no door to enter by, and no floor to walk on, but no doubt Mañjuśrī, being the Bodhisattva of Wisdom, manages to overcome that little problem. On seeing him, Vimalakīrti takes the initiative, calling out

> 'Welcome, Mañjuśrī! You are very welcome! There you are, without any coming. You appear, without any seeing. You are heard, without any hearing.'[43]

Mañjuśrī is not at all disconcerted by this style of greeting; he is quite equal to the occasion. He replies

> 'Householder, it is as you say. Who comes, finally comes not. Who goes, finally goes not. Why? Who comes is not known to come. Who goes is not known to go. Who appears is finally not to be seen.'

Then, having answered Vimalakīrti in his own terms, Mañjuśrī goes on quite coolly to carry out his purpose and ask Vimalakīrti about his sickness. He tells Vimalakīrti that the Buddha has been enquiring after him, and finally he says

> 'Householder, whence came this sickness of yours? How long will it continue? How does it stand? How can it be alleviated?'

These questions take the form of the standard polite Indian enquiries. But Vimalakīrti's reply is not at all standard, and it constitutes one of the most famous and impressive passages in the whole of the *Vimalakīrti-nirdeśa*. He says:

> 'Mañjuśrī, my sickness comes from ignorance and the thirst for existence and it will last as long as do the sicknesses of all living beings. Were all living beings to be free from sickness, I also would not be sick. Why? Mañjuśrī, for the bodhisattva, the world consists only of living beings, and sickness is inherent in living in the world. Were all living beings free of sickness, the bodhisattva also would be free of sickness. For example, Mañjuśrī, when the only son of a

> merchant is sick, both his parents become sick on account of the sickness of their son. And the parents will suffer as long as that only son does not recover from his sickness. Just so, Mañjuśrī, the bodhisattva loves all living beings as if each were his only child. He becomes sick when they are sick and is cured when they are cured. You ask me, Mañjuśrī, whence comes my sickness; the sicknesses of the bodhisattvas arise from great compassion.'[44]

This is Vimalakīrti's reply, and his words resound throughout the history of Mahāyāna Buddhism. But what he is talking about – the Bodhisattva's experience of *mahā-karuṇā*, great Compassion – does present us with an intractable mystery. For us bliss and pain are essentially incompatible. So how does a being who under all circumstances experiences the bliss of liberation also experience the suffering that Vimalakīrti describes? We could say that it is an aspect of experiencing Wisdom and Compassion, *prajñā* and *karuṇā*, as non-different; that is, it is an aspect of the Bodhisattva's compassionate response to suffering as being not different from the same Bodhisattva's profound realization of the emptiness of all things, including living beings and their suffering (and the profound realization itself, of course). We could say that it is an aspect of being in nirvāṇa and *saṁsāra* at the same time. If that is possible, presumably it is possible to experience the bliss of emancipation at the same time that one suffers with beings through great Compassion.

However, we are still in the realm of theory. Perhaps we can find a mundane, if rather faint, analogy for the experience of *mahā-karuṇā* in the way we are able to remain fully absorbed in doing something – like playing a strenuous game – while at the same time receiving some painful knocks. Up to a certain point we don't really notice the pain – or rather we don't take notice of it. It is there, we feel it, but it is very much at the periphery of our consciousness because we are so absorbed in the game and finding it so enjoyable. Perhaps it is not even enjoyment; we are just so caught up in the game that we don't really think about whether we are enjoying it or not.

The Bodhisattva really feels *for* beings rather than suffering *with* them. He certainly doesn't suffer in the same way, or in the same sense, that they do. This is because he is Enlightened, and their suffering is due to their being unenlightened. His 'suffering' is a sympathy rather than an actual experience of suffering. And just as it is impossible actually to experience the toothache that another person experiences, however sympathetic you are, so the Bodhisattva can never experience the suffering of not being Enlightened.

The Bodhisattva's suffering is, in Tennyson's words, a 'painless sympathy with pain', which in a way involves a pain of its own. And this pain is very different, both in quality and in degree, from the kind of sympathy that we might feel. To some people, indeed, a Bodhisattva's sympathy might not seem like sympathy at all, inasmuch as it would not be an indulgent kind of sympathy.

Vimalakīrti's account of the sickness which arises from great Compassion is all very sublime, very deep, very true, very heartfelt – but Mañjuśrī is not satisfied. He is not going to let it rest there. So more brisk dialectical exchanges between Mañjuśrī and Vimalakīrti follow, in the course of which Vimalakīrti becomes very paradoxical indeed.

After this, in reply to another question from Mañjuśrī, Vimalakīrti explains how a Bodhisattva should console another Bodhisattva who is sick. He also explains, at great length, how a sick Bodhisattva should control his mind, and this is followed by a long passage about the nature of the 'domain' of the Bodhisattva. Among Vimalakīrti's many descriptions of this domain, there is this rather baffling specification:

> 'Where one seeks the gnosis of omniscience, yet does not attain this gnosis at the wrong time, there is the domain of the bodhisattva. Where one knows the Four Holy Truths, yet does not realize those truths at the wrong time, there is the domain of the bodhisattva.'[45]

What might this mean? How can there possibly be a wrong time for the realization of the Four Noble Truths, a wrong time for Enlightenment?

The 'wrong time' to 'attain this gnosis' is when the realization is sufficient to gain Arhantship, but not sufficient to gain full Enlightenment. If there is a real distinction between *samyak sambodhi*, supreme Enlightenment, and Arhantship, then you need more wisdom to gain *samyak sambodhi* than to attain Arhantship. And if you are a Bodhisattva, you want to gain *samyak sambodhi*, so you don't develop the gnosis of omniscience as a basis for becoming 'merely' an Arhant. Of course, the whole distinction between *samyak sambodhi* and Arhantship is an artificial one, inasmuch as it is a function of the historical development of the Mahāyāna. But there is a general point to it which holds good: one shouldn't settle down in a partial experience of Enlightenment, even though it may be a genuine experience of Enlightenment so far as it goes. To the extent that there is anything further to realize, one must continue to make an effort. Even the Buddha's Enlightenment was not final; he didn't settle down in a state of realization which thereafter remained the same.

There can't literally be a wrong time for Enlightenment; but there is the possibility that one will settle down in and take as ultimate an experience – whether of 'omniscience' or of the Four Truths – which is in fact only partial. The real mistake is to imagine that Enlightenment represents a sort of conclusion to one's development. If you don't make this mistake then even if you do attain some kind of gnosis, you won't make the mistake of resting on your laurels. You won't think you're Enlightened when you're not. This is what the text is really getting at. And the effect of the whole discourse is such that in eight thousand of those listening to Vimalakīrti the Bodhicitta, 'the spirit of unexcelled, perfect enlightenment' as the text calls it, is awakened.

So the meeting between Vimalakīrti and Mañjuśrī has a dramatic effect; and it continues to do so over the next four chapters of the *Vimalakīrti-nirdeśa*. In fact, their confrontation is one of the main features of the whole work, and it is this that I want now to explore at greater length: the figures of Mañjuśrī and Vimalakīrti, facing each other just as I saw them in that ancient Chinese mural in 1956.

This meeting is more than a confrontation. It is a vigorous dialectical exchange in which neither Bodhisattva spares the other. In a sense each is out to win, to defeat the other – but not in an egoistic way. Each is testing the other, just as a potter tests an earthenware pot to see whether it is cracked. In this confrontation each experiences or tests the other; at the same time, each experiences or tests himself in contact with the other. Each experiences the truth, the reality, of the situation.

The contest between them therefore takes place within a context that is completely positive. Blake says 'Opposition is true friendship.' Friendship, especially spiritual friendship, is not sentimental and indulgent. It is vigorous, challenging, demanding, bracing, invigorating, stimulating – like a cold shower, not a warm bath. In the last chapter we saw Vimalakīrti offering this kind of vigorous friendship to the various Arhants and Bodhisattvas. They were not quite able to stand up to it – it was rather too much for them – but Mañjuśrī is equal to the challenge. The two are in fact more or less evenly matched – so they can be friends.

Nietzsche takes Blake's *aperçu* even further, saying that one's enemies are really one's friends. The greater the enemy, the better the friend. Towards the end of chapter 6 of the *Vimalakīrti-nirdeśa* Vimalakīrti himself says much the same thing in his own way. Mahākāśyapa, one of the Arhants, has just exclaimed

> 'What could the entire host of Māras [the evil ones] ever do to one who is devoted to this inconceivable liberation?'

To which Vimalakīrti replies:

> 'Reverend Mahākāśyapa [they are always very polite to each other in these Mahāyāna texts], the Māras who play the devil in the innumerable universes of the ten directions are all bodhisattvas dwelling in the inconceivable liberation, who are playing the devil in order to develop living beings through their skill in liberative technique. Reverend Mahākāśyapa, all the miserable beggars who come to the bodhisattvas of the innumerable universes of the ten directions to ask for a hand, a foot, an ear, a nose, some blood [they do all these things in the Jātaka stories], muscles, bones, marrow, an eye, a torso, a head, a limb, a member, a throne, a kingdom, a country, a wife, a son, a daughter, a slave, a slave-girl, a horse, an elephant, a chariot, a cart, gold, silver, jewels, pearls, conches, crystal, coral, beryl, treasures, food, drink, elixirs, and clothes – these demanding beggars are usually bodhisattvas living in the inconceivable liberation who, through their skill in liberative technique, wish to test and thus demonstrate the firmness of the high resolve of the bodhisattvas. Why? Reverend Mahākāśyapa, the bodhisattvas demonstrate that firmness by means of terrible austerities. Ordinary persons have no power to be thus demanding of bodhisattvas, unless they are granted the opportunity. They are not capable of killing and depriving in that manner without being freely given the chance.
>
> 'Reverend Mahākāśyapa, just as a glowworm cannot eclipse the light of the sun, so, reverend Mahākāśyapa, it is not possible without special allowance that an ordinary person can thus attack and deprive a bodhisattva. Reverend Mahākāśyapa, just as a donkey could not muster an attack on a wild elephant, even so, reverend Mahākāśyapa, one who is not himself a bodhisattva cannot harass a bodhisattva. Only one who is himself a bodhisattva can harass another bodhisattva.... Reverend Mahākāśyapa, such is the introduction to the power of the knowledge of liberative technique of the bodhisattvas who live in the inconceivable liberation.'[46]

In the last chapter we saw how Indra, the king of the gods, approached the Bodhisattva Jagatīṁdhara and offered him twelve thousand heavenly maidens, which Jagatīṁdhara refused – and how Vimalakīrti came along and said that it was not Indra at all but Māra, the evil one. But in the light of this passage it seems we can go even further than that. Yes,

'Indra' was Māra. But – and this is a question we must put aside as simply a subject for reflection – who was Māra?

The positive aspects of confrontation explain why Vimalakīrti and Mañjuśrī represent what I have called history *versus* myth in our quest for meaning. But what do I mean by our quest for meaning? And we might well ask – as modern scholars, critics, and philosophers have asked – what 'meaning' means in any case. It is not even altogether self-evident what we mean by 'history' and 'myth'. And how does history oppose myth? We shall be going into these questions, but we shall not be going into them very systematically or directly. We shall simply be bringing out some of the implications of the scene depicted in that mural painting. The painting itself is the real answer, the direct answer; that is, the answers are to be sought and found in terms of vision and imagination.

Let us start with the figure of Vimalakīrti. First of all, he is an old man. He has a long white wispy beard, even long white wispy eyebrows, and a puckered, wrinkled, but cheerful and humorous old face. It is quite obvious that he is subject to the process of time – as are we all, even though we might not be wrinkled and white-haired (with or without the wispy beard) – yet.

Not only is Vimalakīrti subject to time, he also lives at a particular point in time. He lives at the time of the Buddha, which according to modern scholarship is the sixth century BCE. He's also subject to space. He lives in a particular part of the world, in the great Indian mercantile city of Vaiśālī. He lives in a particular part of the city, in a particular house (even though at the beginning of chapter 5 he makes it disappear). He has a particular personal identity. He is known by a particular name and belongs to a particular social group. He follows a particular occupation (being apparently engaged in some sort of business), and has, or appears to have, a wife and children. Vimalakīrti thus has a historical personality, a historical existence, an existence which is specific, concrete, contingent, an existence which is determined by time, space, and causality. Vimalakīrti therefore represents historical reality. This does not necessarily mean, incidentally, that he actually existed; this is indeed a matter for dispute among modern Western scholars. What it means is that Vimalakī rti is depicted in the *Vimalakīrti-nirdeśa* as a historical personality.

Mañjuśrī, on the other hand, is a young man. In fact, he is eternally young; that is, he is not subject to the process of time, he does not live at any particular point in time. Nor is he subject to space. He doesn't live in any part of the world. (Chinese Buddhists did try to locate him on Mount Wu-t'ai, one of the five sacred mountains of Buddhist China, but their attempt was not very successful.) However, while he is not bound to any particular time or place, he can *appear* at any time and in any place. Moreover, while Mañjuśrī has a particular personal identity, it is not a mundane identity. His name is a no-name. He doesn't belong to any particular group, doesn't follow any particular occupation. He just does, as occasion arises, whatever is necessary to help living beings develop. And he certainly doesn't have even the semblance of a wife and children.

Mañjuśrī thus has no historical existence. He is not a historical personality. He has an existence which in a manner of speaking is specific and concrete, but which is not contingent, not determined by time, space, or causality. He has what may be called a transcendental existence, a glorified individuality, as his physical appearance suggests. He is not only young but extremely beautiful; he is clad in silks and jewels, and his entire body is surrounded by an aura of brilliant golden light. Mañjuśrī therefore represents supra-historical or archetypal reality; he represents myth. Myth, that is, understood loosely, rather than in any literal sense of the word. In fact, the word does not really have a literal sense. In recent times a whole industry has been set up to explain the meaning of ancient myths; but myths cannot really be explained or understood in a conceptual sense. The meaning of myths, of myth in general, has to be felt, experienced, enacted – lived.

If you take a myth in the modern, sophisticated sense, it has its effect on you, but if you are able to believe that the myth is literally true, it has a much greater effect. For instance, if you are a Christian and you believe that the resurrection of Christ has a deep symbolical significance, even though he didn't literally rise from the dead, the resurrection is a very meaningful symbol for you. But if as an orthodox Christian you believe that Christ literally rose from the dead because he was the son of God and he had that power inherent in him, your belief will have much deeper foundations, or at least you will be more strongly motivated. The nature of our approach to 'myth' is one of the basic questions that have to be faced nowadays, not only by Christians but by Buddhists as well.

For Buddhists, however, it is not such a key issue, because in Buddhism, especially early Buddhism, the taking of myth as literal truth doesn't occupy such an important place. If you read, for example, that the Buddha walked up and down in the air emitting water and fire at the same time, you can believe that quite literally and no doubt find it inspiring. But taking that myth – if it is a myth – literally doesn't occupy the kind of central place in Buddhism that belief in the resurrection of Christ occupies in Christianity. There is no doubt, however, that if you are able to take myth as being literally true, you are likely to practise your religion more zealously and energetically. Of course, such literal belief can go to the undesirable extreme of fanatical fundamentalism. But in avoiding that, perhaps we need to take care not to fall into too sophisticated or rational an approach to myth. The whole point about the realm of myth is that it is a realm not of clearly defined meanings, but of undefined, even indefinable meanings. To this realm also belong such things as symbols, archetypal images, the imagination itself, and poetry.

But just where does Mañjuśrī come from? Where does myth come from? We need be in no doubt about Vimalakīrti's origin; like Gautama the Buddha, he is represented as a historical personality playing his part on the stage of history. But the figure of Mañjuśrī requires some explanation. He is not found in the Pali scriptures. How did he get into Buddhism? How did he get into the pages of the *Vimalakīrti-nirdeśa*? How did he get into the Buddha's assembly?

We can begin to answer this question by reaching back to the Pali scriptures, which are the records of the Buddha's teaching kept by the Theravāda or 'School of Elders', one of the earliest schools of Buddhism. Although these scriptures were not written down until several hundred years after the Buddha's *parinirvāṇa*, the oldest parts of them undoubtedly reflect, at least to some extent, the conditions under which Gautama the Buddha lived and taught, and the form that his teachings assumed. We find in them a great deal of information about the political situation, social conditions, economic life, manners and customs, religious beliefs and superstitions prevalent in the India of the Buddha's time. They are in fact our main source of information about northern India during this period. The result is that in the Pali scriptures we find the Dharma deeply embedded in its historical context, even overlaid to some extent by that context. We find a Buddhism which is a historical phenomenon; a Buddhism which is determined by time, space, and causality; a Buddhism which exists and expresses itself in terms of historical reality, but which is also obscured and concealed by that historical reality.

Like the figure of Vimalakīrti, the Buddhism of the Pali scriptures belongs to the realm of historical rather than archetypal reality. It is true that some elements of myth are found in the Pali scriptures, but these are found in a rudimentary though still very beautiful form, mainly in parables and extended similes. By contrast, the elements of historical reality found in the Mahāyāna sūtras occupy a distinctly subordinate place. For instance, in the *Vimalakīrti-nirdeśa* we find ourselves in Āmrapālī's Garden and in the city of Vaiśālī, but into this realm of homely historical reality there irrupts the realm of archetypal, even spiritual, reality. Or, to put it another way, the realm of homely historical reality is made to open up in all directions into the realm of archetypal reality, as when Vimalakīrti or the Buddha performs a miracle or puts on a display of magical power.

The origins of the Mahāyāna sūtras lie partly in the dissatisfaction of some early Buddhists with the Pali scriptures. They were not satisfied with the expression of Buddhism in terms of historical reality. They were not interested – as nowadays we only too often are interested – in Buddhism as a historical phenomenon. The notion of history in the modern sense was in any case probably quite unknown to them. For them, the Dharma really was *sanāntana*, eternal. They wanted to free it from its historical context, to emancipate it from the limitations of a merely historical existence.

They were interested, we could say, in what the Buddha said rather than in the historical conditions under which he said it. They were committed to the Dharma as a living spiritual reality. Consequently, they tended to forget the historical situation in which the Buddha lived and taught. It didn't seem very important to them. Instead, they concentrated more and more on the Buddha as a purely spiritual personality, and on the Dharma as a purely spiritual truth whose deeper implications they sought to bring out.

Thus they sought not only to emancipate the Dharma from the limitations of history, but also to universalize it, to reformulate it in such a way as to make it applicable not just to the people of northern India in the sixth century BCE, but to all living beings throughout time and throughout space. This was, of course, implicit in the Dharma as the Buddha taught it. He taught it, after all, *bahujana hitāya, bahujana sukhāya*, 'for the welfare and happiness of many people'. But the forebears of the Mahayanists felt that the universal quality of Buddhism needed to be made more explicit. This dehistoricizing, universalizing, idealizing tendency was one aspect of the development of what later came to be known as the Mahāyāna, which eventually found expression in the Mahāyāna scriptures.

Another element the Mahayanists brought to the teachings was a love of adornment and decoration. A friend of mine once remarked 'That which we love, we adorn.' If this is true, the Mahāyāna scriptures show us how very much those who originated them must have loved the Dharma, because they adorned it magnificently. They set it in an ideal, archetypal realm, flashing with light and glowing with all the colours of the rainbow, a realm where everything was made of jewels, and the air was filled with music and perfume. In short, they transferred the Dharma from the realm of historical reality to the realm of spiritual reality, from the realm of history to the realm of what I have called myth.

We can see this process most clearly, perhaps, in the development of the figure of the Buddha himself. In the Pali scriptures the Buddha appears as a wandering religious mendicant. The texts describe him as 'shaven-headed', but we must not imagine him with a shiny pate; his head and chin were probably covered in a heavy stubble. His 'robes' were not the bright, carefully laundered garb of the modern bhikkhu, but ochre-coloured rags. He carried a wooden or metal begging-bowl. From a distance he must have been indistinguishable from the thousands of other wandering ascetics who thronged India in his time – and still do today. The Pali scriptures themselves describe occasions on which the Buddha was not recognized by other people, even by bhikkhus at close quarters.

But it is impossible to mistake the Buddha of the Mahāyāna for anyone else. As he appears in the Mahāyāna scriptures, he is seated on a lofty, elaborate, jewelled throne with a canopy of jewels suspended, glittering, above his head. The begging-bowl in his lap appears to be carved from a solid block of lapis-lazuli or emerald, and a brilliant golden light radiates from his head and body. He teaches the Dharma not just for a few hours, or a few years, or the span of a human life, but for age upon age without pause. He teaches it in a purely spiritual or archetypal realm, to hundreds of thousands, even millions, of living beings. Some of these beings – like Arhants such as Ānanda – are figures familiar to us from the Pali scriptures, but others are not familiar to us at all. And among these unfamiliar figures are the Bodhisattvas, including, of course, Mañjuśrī.

So if you read the Pali scriptures and then the Mahāyāna scriptures – say two or three volumes of each, enough to give you a taste of them – you will notice that you get something from the Mahāyāna scriptures that is completely missing from the Pali texts. This is not by any means to dismiss the unique historical and spiritual importance of the Pali scriptures. They give us a vivid and deeply moving picture of the life and teaching career of the human historical Buddha. They contain all the basic spiritual principles and practices from which all the subsequent forms of Buddhism developed. They are rich in content and full of inspiration. We cannot possibly dispense with the Pali scriptures; as Buddhists, we are enormously indebted to them. Humanity, in fact, is indebted to them. They cannot be praised enough and we cannot be sufficiently grateful for them.

They do not, however, contain everything that everybody needs. There is an element missing, and it is this element that we find in the Mahāyāna scriptures. Reading the Mahāyāna scriptures, we are emancipated from the contingent and the determinate, from time, space, and causality, from historical reality. We experience archetypal reality, myth, the realm of undefined meanings. In technical terms, we encounter the *sambhogakāya*. That is, we encounter the Buddhas and Bodhisattvas of the Mahāyāna in their archetypal forms. Through this experience we contact something within us of which we were not previously aware. Something is sparked off that even the Pali scriptures were unable to spark off. And this happens because the realm of archetypal reality, of myth, of undefined meanings, corresponds to something within us.

According to the *Tibetan Book of the Dead*, we experience this realm directly when we die. In the intermediate state between death and rebirth we experience all sorts of visions, including visions of Buddhas and Bodhisattvas in both their peaceful and their wrathful forms. And the Buddhist tradition tells us not to be afraid, but to recognize all these visions, all these Buddhas and Bodhisattvas, as our own thought forms, as phenomena of our own true mind. If we can do this, we attain liberation on the spot.

As a writer, one inevitably notices a difference in feeling between the experience of composing passages of conceptual prose and the experience of writing something more creative, more inspired or poetic. It is this kind of shift we feel when we make the transition from the prose of the Pali scriptures to the poetry of the Mahāyāna scriptures, the transition from history to myth on a grand scale.

Unfortunately, some people cannot make this transition. Take the well-known case of Charles Darwin. As a young man Darwin loved poetry and literature, especially Shakespeare, but for the greater part of his life he immersed himself in scientific research. When as an old man he tried to get back to Shakespeare, he found to his dismay that poetry held no meaning for him any more; he had lost his capacity to enjoy it. In the course of his years, even decades, of scientific research a whole side of him had withered and died. Much the same happened to John Stuart Mill, at least for part of his life. Even as a small boy his favourite subjects were logic and political economy; and as he grew older he found that he became more and more cut off from poetry. It is not just that he was cut off from poetry in the literary sense; he was – to put it rather poetically – cut off from the poetry of life.

Today we are all exposed to this sort of danger. We all suffer from this sort of deprivation, at least to some extent. We have been suffering from it, in fact, since the Industrial Revolution, at the beginning of which William Blake warned against the loss of what he called 'the divine vision'. He criticized Bacon, Newton, and Locke so vigorously because he felt that they tended to limit humanity to the realm of historical reality, the realm of time, space, and causality. In his own literary and visual creative work Blake, of course, was not limited in this way. In his Prophetic Books especially he explores the deeper levels of human experience. Blake's profound concern with archetypal forces and forms must explain why he continues to hold such a great fascination for so many people today.

Our desire to contact the realm of the archetypal also explains the popularity of tales of myth and fantasy, whether traditional, like the stories of King Arthur, or modern, like *The Lord of the Rings* and some forms of science fiction. Such works explore facets of humanity's quest for meaning, and in reading them we are trying, perhaps unconsciously, to break out of the prison of merely historical reality, seeking to experience a deeper meaning to our existence.

Meaning is not a thing that you can grasp by looking in a dictionary. Meaning must be meaning *for you*, something that you personally experience. Our quest for meaning is therefore our quest for ourselves, our quest for the totality, the wholeness, of our own being. On one level we belong to the realm of historical reality; but on another, we belong to the realm of spiritual reality. The Mahāyāna scriptures reveal this world to us. So does myth; so does poetry. And they reveal it to us not as something external to ourselves, but as our own world, as a world in which we ourselves actually live, usually without knowing it.

It was a maxim of the Neoplatonists that the eye could not behold the sun unless it had within its nature something sun-like, something akin to the sun.[47] Similarly, we can experience the archetypal realm only because we ourselves are, on another level, archetypal beings. If we really allow ourselves to become absorbed in a Mahāyāna sūtra, we become part of it. We join the great assembly and experience ourselves right in the midst of it, taking part in the events of the sūtra as they unfold.

But although we can make the transition to the realm of archetypal reality, this does not mean that we leave the realm of historical reality behind. We cannot – must not – opt for myth and discard history. We need both – because we exist in both realms. We exist in them both all the time, whether or not we are aware of it. And of course a lot of the time we are not aware of it. Our relation to the archetypal realm is analogous to our relation to the dream state. When we are asleep and dreaming, we exist, one might say, in the dream realm, and we have all sorts of experiences. When we wake up, we are no longer in the dream state, but the emotions we experienced while we were dreaming continue. It's just like an underground river that we descend into from time to time through a hole in the ground. Just as the river is flowing all the time, so there is continuity between dreams. You can even have a dream, wake up, and then fall asleep again and continue with the same dream, as though it has been going on all the time.

So in a sense we are living in that dream realm all the time. And we can extend that to the realm of archetypal experience. Just as a very strong dream continues to have its effect when we have woken up, so the archetypal realm continues to affect us, whether or not we are conscious of it. There is no question, therefore, of our literally passing from one realm to the other. They do not even exist side by side. In the mural painting Vimalakīrti and Mañjuśrī *confront* one another in a vigorous encounter. This is history *versus* myth – and what we have to do is bring them together. There has to be a sort of 'marriage' between Vimalakīrti and Mañjuśrī. We have to realize that Vimalakīrti *is* Mañjuśrī, and Mañjuśrī *is* Vimalakīrti. Time is eternity; eternity is time. *Rūpa* is *śūnyatā*; *śūnyatā* is *rūpa*. If we can realize that, then history *and* myth will have played their part in humanity's quest for meaning; and that quest for meaning – our quest for ourselves – will be complete.

6

The Way of Non-duality

So Mañjuśrī and Vimalakīrti confront each other in Vimalakīrti's 'empty' house in Vaiśālī. In front of an audience of thousands upon thousands of Bodhisattvas, Arhants, gods, and goddesses, they discourse profoundly on the sickness of Bodhisattvas and living beings, on the nature of emptiness, and on the domain of the Bodhisattvas, where all extremes, all dualities, are transcended. The entire company is spellbound by their eloquence. In fact, in eight thousand gods and goddesses the Bodhicitta – the will towards supreme perfect Enlightenment for the sake of all living beings – is awakened.

And yet, at the beginning of chapter 6, 'The Inconceivable Liberation', our friend Śāriputra has a problem. There is now an immense crowd in Vimalakīrti's house – but all the furniture has disappeared. Where is everybody going to sit? After all, Śāriputra is perhaps thinking, according to ancient Indian etiquette, no guest of whatever kind should be kept standing. Bodhisattvas and Arhants should certainly not have to remain standing while Vimalakīrti is lying on his couch, even though he is sick.

As we know, Vimalakīrti has the disconcerting faculty of telepathy. Knowing Śāriputra's thoughts, he puts to him a rather pointed question:

> 'Reverend Śāriputra, did you come here for the sake of the Dharma? Or did you come here for the sake of a chair?'

Well, you can imagine Śāriputra's feelings! He very humbly replies:

> 'I came for the sake of the Dharma, not for the sake of a chair.'

But Vimalakīrti continues, saying:

> 'Reverend Śāriputra, he who is interested in the Dharma is not interested even in his own body, much less in a chair.'[48]

And, no doubt to Śāriputra's great embarrassment, he presses the point home, carrying on in this vein for several paragraphs.

But Vimalakīrti's initial question gives us quite enough to think about. We may be tempted to smile at poor old Śāriputra. Here we have a great assembly of Bodhisattvas, Arhants, and all sorts of extraordinary beings. The wise elder Vimalakīrti and Mañjuśrī, the Bodhisattva of Wisdom himself, have just had a discussion of tremendous spiritual significance. Everybody has been highly delighted and uplifted by it, and they are all wondering what is going to happen next. And Śāriputra starts worrying about chairs....

But if we find Śāriputra's behaviour a source of amusement, we should also be able to look to our own behaviour for further amusement, because this little incident warns us against a danger to which we are all liable – the danger of getting sidetracked. Say we attend a meditation class, or a lecture on the Dharma, or perhaps even go away on retreat into the depths of the countryside. We may get quite deeply absorbed in our meditation, or engaged in the lecture, or immersed in the retreat experience – but sooner or later our attention wanders. We start wondering when the tea and biscuits are going to appear, or whether a certain attractive person we saw last week will be there, or whether the central heating is going to be turned up.

We might well ask ourselves the kind of question that Vimalakīrti asked Śāriputra. 'Did I come for the sake of the Dharma or did I come for the sake of the tea and biscuits?' 'Did I come for the sake of the Dharma or for the sake of seeing that attractive person?' 'Did I come for the sake of the Dharma or for the sake of the central heating?' There is nothing easier than to get sidetracked in this way, to succumb to the gravitational pull of the conditioned. We have a deeply ingrained tendency to be over-concerned with the mundane, the trivial, the everyday, at the expense of our spiritual development: in a word, to be over-concerned with comfort.

Before we move on, it is worth bearing in mind that the Śāriputra who appears in the *Vimalakīrti-nirdeśa* is not the same figure as the relatively historical Śāriputra (or rather Sāriputta) that we encounter in the pages of the Pali scriptures. Historically, Śāriputra was one of the two most prominent disciples of the Buddha Śākyamuni (the other being Mahā-Maudgalyāyana) and he was renowned as the wisest teacher of the Dharma after the Buddha himself. But in the Mahāyāṇa sūtras he came to represent the narrow, rather literalistic attitude which had developed in some Buddhist circles, and which the Mahāyāna tried to correct. We should therefore bear in mind that the *Vimalakīrti-nirdeśa* uses the figure of Śāriputra, both here and in several other places, in an imaginative rather than a historically factual manner. As Thurman puts it, perhaps rather crudely, he is used as a 'fall guy' to express the limited Hīnayāna view so that it can then be exposed by the Buddha, or by Vimalakīrti or some other Bodhisattva. He also seems liable, as in this particular instance, to be prey to petty and mundane anxieties.

So Śāriputra is worried about chairs. All right, Vimalakīrti gives him chairs: thirty-two-hundred-thousand of them. And they are not ordinary chairs, but lion-thrones, brought by Vimalakīrti's magical power from a distant Buddha-land in the eastern direction, whence, according to Mañjuśrī, the best lion-thrones come. And all these thrones fit into Vimalakīrti's house without crowding; it seems to grow to accommodate them. And not only the house needs to grow. All the thrones are thirty-four-hundred-thousand leagues high, and the visitors have to be helped to enlarge their own bodies so that they can take advantage of these unusual seating arrangements. Perhaps not surprisingly, the Arhants have more difficulty than the Bodhisattvas, but this is soon overcome. Śāriputra remarks how astonishing the whole business is, and this gives Vimalakīrti the opportunity to explain the inconceivable emancipation, the state of emancipation in which a Bodhisattva – through comprehending fully the relativity of space and time – can bring about all sorts of magical transformations.

In chapter 7, entitled 'The Goddess', Śāriputra is in trouble again. First of all though, Mañjuśrī asks Vimalakīrti how a Bodhisattva should regard all living beings, and Vimalakīrti replies in a series of beautiful similes which illustrate how a Bodhisattva should regard beings in order to realize that they are ultimately selfless or insubstantial. They are like the reflection of the moon in water, the sound of an echo, a flash of lightning, a face in the mirror, and so on. But if a Bodhisattva considers all beings in this way, Mañjuśrī wants to know, how does he generate love towards them? And Vimalakīrti speaks very movingly about the nature of the loving kindness, the mettā, that the Bodhisattva feels. After this poetic exchange, there follows another vigorous dialectical debate between the two Bodhisattvas.

At this point a certain goddess appears. She lives, apparently, in Vimalakīrti's house and she is so delighted with the teaching she has been hearing that she showers the whole assembly – the Arhants, the Bodhisattvas, everybody – with flowers. In the case of the Arhants – who being monks are not supposed to decorate themselves – the flowers become uncharacteristically and embarrassingly sticky. Despite his best efforts to brush them off, Śāriputra remains spectacularly adorned.

The goddess explains that the flowers do not stick to the bodies of the Bodhisattvas because they – the Bodhisattvas – have no attachment to discriminative views and thought-constructions. This leads to an exchange of views in which Śāriputra, as usual, comes off worst, and is at one point completely lost for words. A little later on he finds himself still more embarrassed when, to make a point about the relativity of manifesting as a man or as a woman, the goddess causes him to undergo a change of sex. First of all he changes from male to female, which is bad enough in his opinion, and then from female back to male, which is even worse. I am making fun of Śāriputra here, but the point is that undergoing a sex change from male to female really should have alerted him to the relativity of gender. But instead of becoming androgynous as a result of this experience, he remains within the dichotomy of gender – so when he returns to his original gender, he still hasn't really learned anything.

This incident has rather a modern ring to it, of course, in an era when having a 'sex change' in a literal sense is possible. From a spiritual point of view, I doubt very much whether having a sex change would help anyone to transcend the dichotomy of gender; those who have had such an operation often seem to have the experience of feeling trapped by it. Such changes represent alternation, not integration. Spiritually speaking, what is important is for a man to incorporate the so-called feminine psychological qualities, and for a woman to incorporate the so-called masculine ones – in addition to those proper to one's own physical-cum-psychological gender. This would be true androgyny, for which there could never be an operation. The surgeons might be able to make someone a hermaphrodite, but they could never make anyone genuinely androgynous.

Śāriputra's double 'sex change' happens in the space of a few minutes; and the chapter ends with Vimalakīrti praising the goddess as an irreversible Bodhisattva. Chapter 8 is entitled 'The Family of the Tathāgatas' – that is, the family of the Buddhas. Replying to yet another question from Mañjuśrī, Vimalakīrti explains, in his usual highly paradoxical fashion, how the Bodhisattva follows 'the way to attain the qualities of the Buddha'. Vimalakīrti himself then puts a question to Mañjuśrī, asking him what is meant by the expression 'family of the Tathāgatas'. Mañjuśrī's response is also highly paradoxical, and it is praised at some length by Mahākāśyapa.

Following this discussion of families, a Bodhisattva called Sarvarūpasaṁdharśana ('Universal Manifestation') then asks Vimalakīrti a whole string of questions about his own family:

> 'Householder, where are your father and mother, your children, your wife,'

– remember that Vimalakīrti is lying there on his couch and nobody else can be seen –

> 'your servants, your maids, your laborers, and your attendants? Where are your friends, your relatives, and your kinsmen? Where are your servants, your horses, your elephants, your chariots, your bodyguards, and your bearers?'[49]

Vimalakīrti replies to this typically Indian enquiry in a long series of beautiful verses, over forty of them. They last until the end of the chapter and comprise the longest verse passage in the *Vimalakīrti-nirdeśa*. Here, just to give a taste of them, are the first twelve:

Of the true bodhisattvas,
The mother is the transcendence of wisdom,
The father is the skill in liberative technique;
The Leaders are born of such parents.

Their wife is the joy in the Dharma,
Love and compassion are their daughters,
The Dharma and the truth are their sons;
And their home is deep thought on the meaning of voidness.

All the passions are their disciples,
Controlled at will.
Their friends are the aids to enlightenment;
Thereby they realize supreme enlightenment.

Their companions, ever with them,
Are the six transcendences.
Their consorts are the means of unification,
Their music is the teaching of the Dharma.

The incantations make their garden,
Which blossoms with the flowers of the factors of enlightenment,
With trees of the great wealth of the Dharma,
And fruits of the gnosis of liberation.

Their pool consists of the eight liberations,
Filled with the water of concentration,
Covered with the lotuses of the seven purities –
Who bathes therein becomes immaculate.

Their bearers are the six superknowledges,
Their vehicle is the unexcelled Mahāyāna,
Their driver is the spirit of enlightenment,
And their path is the eightfold peace.

Their ornaments are the auspicious signs,
And the eighty marks;
Their garland is virtuous aspiration,
And their clothing is good conscience and consideration.

Their wealth is the holy Dharma,
And their business is its teaching,
Their great income is pure practice,
And it is dedicated to the supreme enlightenment.

Their bed consists of the four contemplations,
And its spread is the pure livelihood,
And their awakening consists of gnosis,
Which is constant learning and meditation.

Their food is the ambrosia of the teachings,
And their drink is the juice of liberation.
Their bath is pure aspiration,
And morality their unguent and perfume.

Having conquered the enemy passions,
They are the invincible heroes.
Having subdued the four Māras,
They raise their standard on the field of enlightenment.[50]

In this way we come to chapter 9, 'The Dharma Door of Non-Duality'. The structure of this chapter is very simple. Vimalakīrti asks the Bodhisattvas a question, to which thirty-one of them in turn give answers. The same question is then put by the Bodhisattvas to Mañjuśrī, and by Mañjuśrī to Vimalakīrti, and each of them answers it in his own way. The question Vimalakīrti asks is 'Please explain how the bodhisattvas enter the Dharma-door of nonduality.'

Now, what kind of question is this? To begin with, what is meant by the expression 'Dharma-door'? It is a term which occurs frequently in Mahāyāna texts – *dharma-mukha* is the Sanskrit expression. In this context, *dharma* has its usual meaning – the teaching or the doctrine of the Buddha – and *mukha* is 'door', 'entrance', 'opening', or 'mouth'. The Dharma is a door in the sense that it is a means of access to the ultimate truth, to the experience of Enlightenment. But a door, any door, has a twofold function. It can open into something, but it can also shut something out. In the same way, the Dharma is a means of entrance into ultimate truth when it is approached as a means to an end, but it shuts you out from ultimate truth when it is taken as an end in itself. If you regard it as an end in itself, the door – or what should have been the door – becomes just part of the wall. You may even forget that it was ever meant for going through. Furthermore, the word Dharma itself has a double meaning. As well as meaning the teaching or doctrine, it also means the truth or reality indicated by that teaching or doctrine. So the Dharma is the door to the Dharma: the Dharma as teaching is the door to the Dharma as reality – provided it is not taken as an end in itself.

To return to Vimalakīrti's question: How do the Bodhisattvas enter the Dharma-door of non-duality? What *is* the Bodhisattva's Dharma-door of non-duality? The Dharma as teaching or doctrine is expressed in concepts, and every concept you can think of has an opposite. If there is truth, there must be falsehood. If there is brightness, there must be darkness. The Dharma is therefore always expressed, whether explicitly or implicitly, in terms of pairs of opposites – that is, in terms of duality. The Yogācāra, a philosophical school of Mahāyāna Buddhism, offers a reason for this. It says that concepts are the creation of the *kliśto-mano-vijñāna* or 'defiled-mind-consciousness', which sees everything, even Reality itself, in terms of pairs of opposites. But in the experience of Reality, all duality is transcended, even the duality between duality and non-duality. Reality is *advaya*, non-dual. In Reality, duality is not obliterated – one is not left with a blank featureless unity – for there can be no question of obliterating something which in reality does not exist.

We ourselves are creatures of duality. Our consciousness is dualistic; our experience is dualistic; our thoughts, words, and deeds are dualistic; our understanding and practice of the Dharma is dualistic. The Dharma itself is expressed in terms of concepts which are pairs of opposites: skilful and unskilful; mundane and transcendental; conditioned and unconditioned; bondage and liberation; defilement and purity. We have to use dualistic expressions as a means of realizing non-dual Reality; we have no alternative. And in fact it works because in Reality there is no absolute duality between duality and non-duality. If this were not true, no emancipation would be possible.

But how in practice can we realize non-duality by means of the dualistic? This is what Vimalakīrti is getting at in his question to the Bodhisattvas. How do the Bodhisattvas make a dualistic Dharma function in a non-dualistic way? Being themselves riddled with dualism, how do they follow the way of non-duality?

It's a good question, and the Bodhisattvas, one by one, set about answering it. Each Bodhisattva, speaking from his own point of view, states a pair of opposites, a duality, and then shows how, by means of the contradictions inherent in it, that duality can be transcended in terms of itself.

For example, the Bodhisattva Bhadrajyotis says

> '"Distraction" and "attention" are two. When there is no distraction, there will be no attention, no mentation, and no mental intensity. Thus, the absence of mental intensity is the entrance into nonduality.'[51]

This is Thurman's translation. Lamotte's version makes the meaning a little clearer: 'Distraction and attention are two. If there is no distraction, there is neither attention nor reflection nor interest. This absence of interest is the entry into non-duality.'[52]

The word used for distraction is *vikṣepa,* which means distraction in the sense of floundering: the floundering, the tossing, the wandering of the mind. And the word for attention is *manyanā* in the sense of 'paying attention'. We could also perhaps render the word as 'concentration' but it is not quite the same thing. *Manyanā* is more like what makes concentration possible.

This pair of opposites is experienced especially within the context of meditation, as anybody who practises meditation knows very well. What usually happens is that we begin by paying attention to our object of concentration – breath, mantra, whatever it may be. But after a while the mind gets restless. It feels uncomfortable and starts to wander. Sooner or later we become aware of what has happened – what *is* happening – and we start paying attention again. In this way we oscillate between the two: distraction and attention, distraction and attention. This is how our meditation proceeds.

If we are to learn to concentrate in meditation, we will have to find the doorway to non-duality. We have to question the very terms of the situation – or rather, question the absoluteness of those terms. We have to realize that it is not enough to try to sustain attention by means of a forcible act of will. If distractions persistently arise when we are meditating, we have not understood ourselves deeply enough. There are psychological factors at work within us of which we are not conscious. We need, therefore, to become conscious of them, to take them into consideration – in a word, to become more integrated. When we are more integrated, the different elements of our being will no longer be in conflict with one another, and we will no longer have to oscillate between them, because they will all pull in the same direction.

So in the case of distraction and attention, integration is the entry into non-duality. Integration within the context of meditation practice is not synonymous with the experience of non-duality in the highest sense, but it is certainly a step in that direction. This does not mean that we should never try to concentrate, never try to get rid of distractions. That may be necessary as a provisional measure – in fact, it almost certainly will be. And some meditation practices – the mindfulness of breathing, for example – have an integrating effect. But in the long run the opposition between distraction and attention which plagues so much of our meditation practice can only be resolved if we become more psychologically and emotionally integrated.

Let's take another example. The Bodhisattva Subāhu declares

> '"Bodhisattva-spirit" and "disciple-spirit" are two. When both are seen to resemble an illusory spirit, there is no bodhisattva-spirit, nor any disciple-spirit. Thus, the sameness of natures of spirits is the entrance into nonduality.'[53]

Here, 'spirit' does not mean 'ghost'. It translates the Sanskrit *citta* and means something like 'mental attitude'. Again, Lamotte's translation is clearer: 'Bodhisattva mind and Listener mind are two. If it is seen that these two minds are the same as an illusionary mind, there is neither Bodhisattva mind nor Listener mind. This sameness of the mark of minds is the entry into non-duality.'[54]

'Illusory spirit' or 'illusionary mind' (*māyā-citta* in Sanskrit) is not a mind that is absolutely non-existent, but rather a mind that, like the magical show, cannot be defined in terms of existence or non-existence. It is a relatively real mind which has a relatively real existence, and which sees things in a relatively real way. It corresponds roughly to the *kliśto-mano-vijñāna* or 'defiled-mind consciousness' of the Yogācāra, which sees things in terms of pairs of mutually exclusive opposites: self and other, good and bad, pure and impure, and so on.[55]

One of these pairs of apparent opposites is gaining emancipation for oneself alone, or gaining emancipation for others. If the illusory mind identifies itself with the latter, it becomes the Bodhisattva-mind; if it identifies itself with the former, it becomes the *śrāvaka*-mind, the listener- or disciple-mind. But this distinction is ultimately unreal. You cannot progress spiritually yourself without paying attention to the needs of others, without developing friendliness and compassion. And you cannot help others to progress spiritually unless you have made some progress yourself.

Bodhisattva-mind and disciple-mind, Bodhisattva ideal and Arhant ideal, are not mutually exclusive. The Mahāyāna and the Hīnayāna are not mutually exclusive. Both are products of the illusory, relative, dualistic mind, and both represent attempts on the part of this mind to apprehend the nature of the non-dual spiritual ideal. If we understand the limitations of that mind, we will understand the limitations of Bodhisattva-mind and disciple-mind considered as mutually exclusive. The realization that Bodhisattva-mind and disciple-mind are both the same as illusory mind is the Dharma-door to non-duality. When we use terms like 'Bodhisattva ideal' and 'Arhant ideal' we must realize that they have only a relative validity. They are not ends in themselves; their function is simply to help us grow.

Next, we'll examine a reply concerned with the concept of sin. The Bodhisattva Siṁha says

> '"Sinfulness" and "sinlessness" are two. By means of the diamond-like wisdom that pierces to the quick, not to be bound or liberated is the entrance into nonduality.'[56]

The word translated as 'sinfulness' is *savadya*. Lamotte translates it as 'blame', which is more literal. So, who blames us? Who says we are sinful? It could be the group; it could be an individual. Let's say it is the group. When we are blamed by the group, especially our own group, the group to which we feel we belong, we feel very wretched and miserable indeed.

We may be ready to do almost anything to recapture the group's approval; we are completely at its mercy. The opposites here are praise and blame – we swing between elation when we are not blamed and wretchedness when we are. The situation becomes even worse when God comes into it. Then we may be found not just blameable but actually sinful. But we won't go into all that now – it is too horrible even to think about. What we need to do is find out how to escape the oscillation between praise and blame. The door to non-duality in this case is the development of transcendental individuality, an individuality which is not at the mercy of the group, which is in a sense indifferent to the opinion of the group.

It is difficult enough to develop ordinary individuality. Transcendental individuality can be developed only by means of Wisdom, the transcendental Wisdom that cuts like a diamond, that sees through the power of the group. Ordinary mundane wisdom is not enough. The impact of the group on the individual is strong and persistent, and we cannot help weakening, even giving in, sometimes. Only transcendental individuality is strong enough to resist the pressure, to remain unaffected by the group's opinion. This is quite a sobering thought. It means that until we have entered the Stream[57] – for only then does transcendental individuality begin to develop – we shall continue to swing between praise and blame, between elation and wretchedness, at least to some extent.

No doubt other, more metaphysical interpretations of Siṁha's declaration are possible, but this one seems particularly appropriate to us. And we need not be afraid to place our own interpretations on traditional texts. When told that a rival saint had interpreted a passage in the Bible differently from himself, Saint Augustine apparently said calmly 'The more interpretations the better.' This has always been the view of the Buddhist tradition towards its scriptures: the more interpretations the better. (I might note in passing, however, that this has not always or even usually been the view of the Christian tradition, where differences in interpretation have frequently been the cause of very bitter, even vicious, disputes and persecution.)

To take a fourth and last example, let's look at the declaration of the Bodhisattva Śāntendriya. He says

> 'It is dualistic to say "Buddha", "Dharma", and "Sangha". The Dharma is itself the nature of the Buddha, the Sangha is itself the nature of the Dharma, and all of them are uncompounded [or, as it is more usually expressed, Unconditioned]. The uncompounded is

> infinite space, and the processes of all things are equivalent to infinite space. Adjustment to this is the entrance into nonduality.'[58]

Here we have two pairs of opposites: Buddha and Dharma, Dharma and Sangha. Dharma, the term the two pairs have in common, is here to be taken in the more metaphysical sense: not the Buddha's teaching as expressed in words and concepts, but the ultimate reality of which that teaching is the expression and towards which it points. By virtue of his Enlightenment experience the Buddha is the living embodiment of the Dharma in this sense; so, as Śāntendriya declares, there is no duality between Dharma and Buddha.

We find something similar in the case of the Sangha – that is, the Ārya-Saṅgha, the spiritual community of Bodhisattvas, Arhants, Non-Returners, Once-Returners, and Stream-Entrants. All of them are following the transcendental path, so all of them stand in some relation to the Unconditioned, some nearer, some further away. In some cases they have actually reached it. This means that in principle there is no duality between the Dharma and the Sangha. And if there is no difference between the Buddha and the Dharma, and no difference between the Dharma and the Sangha, there can be no difference between the Buddha and the Sangha. All three essentially *are* the Unconditioned. The Dharma is the Unconditioned itself; the Buddha is the Unconditioned as fully realized by the individual; and the Sangha is the Unconditioned in process of realization.

So in the case of the two pairs of opposites which make up the Three Jewels, the entry into non-duality is the realization that the Buddha, the Dharma, and the Sangha are essentially Unconditioned. So long as we see them as conditioned, we see them as three, but when we see them as Unconditioned, we see them as one. From this point of view, when we go for Refuge to the Three Jewels, we commit ourselves not to three different things, but to one Unconditioned non-dual ultimate Reality.

Now all this may sound rather metaphysical, not to say abstract – although these four examples are among the simpler, less metaphysical of the Bodhisattvas' replies to Vimalakīrti's question. But the general drift is clear enough. Dualities, pairs of opposites – including those pairs of opposites which are the doctrinal categories of Buddhism itself – are created by the mind. One enters the Dharma-door of non-duality when one realizes that all pairs of opposites are created by the mind and that they are therefore not ultimately valid. They are not ends in themselves but means to an end, means to the spiritual development of the individual. Moreover, any pair of opposites whatsoever can be a Dharma-door to non-duality. Duality itself is the means to non-duality, because the duality between duality and non-duality is not ultimate.

This is still, it must be admitted, very much in the realm of the metaphysical. But we can apply the same principle on a much more down-to-earth level, and come up with our own dualities. Here are a few to begin with. They are certainly not so sublime as those of the *Vimalakīrti-nirdeśa*, but no doubt they come somewhat closer to our own experience and as such they may be more useful. They may not carry us as far into the depths of non-duality, but at least they will help us move in that direction from where we are now.

Masculine and feminine are two; individuality is the entrance into non-duality.

Organizer and organized are two; co-operation is the entrance into non-duality.

Teacher and taught are two; communication is the entrance into non-duality.

God and man are two; blasphemy is the entrance into non-duality.

Male and female are two; celibacy is the entrance into non-duality.

Individual and group are two; the spiritual community is the entrance into non-duality.

These are just a few suggestions; no doubt there are many more such dualities to be reflected on. But it is possible to go even further than seeking the entrance to non-duality in any pair of opposites, as Mañjuśrī's reply to Vimalakīrti's question shows. He says

> 'Good sirs, you have all spoken well. Nevertheless, all your explanations are themselves dualistic. To know no one teaching, to express nothing, to say nothing, to explain nothing, to announce nothing, to indicate nothing, and to designate nothing – that is the entrance into non-duality.'[59]

Mañjuśrī means that the Bodhisattvas' explanations are dualistic because they are all expressed in terms of concepts, which are essentially dualistic. We cannot explain the Bodhisattva's entry into non-duality by means of concepts; to explain it, we have to give up concepts altogether. We cannot, therefore, rely on words to explain non-duality. The only thing we can do is remain completely silent.

But to explain this, Mañjuśrī himself has resorted to speech. He has *said* that silence is the Bodhisattva's entry into non-duality. So Mañjuśrī's explanation itself is not entirely free from duality. There is still one more step to be taken – and Vimalakīrti takes it.

> Then, the crown prince Mañjuśrī said to the Licchavi Vimalakīrti, 'We have all given our own teachings, noble sir. Now, may you elucidate the teaching of the entrance into the principle of non-duality!'
>
> Thereupon, the Licchavi Vimalakīrti kept his silence, saying nothing at all.[60]

Vimalakīrti remains completely silent. He puts into actual practice what Mañjuśrī has only expressed in terms of concepts. This is the famous 'thunder-like' silence of Vimalakīrti, the silence that is more powerful, more expressive, than any words. And it represents not only the climax of the chapter, but surely the climax of the entire *Vimalakīrti-nirdeśa*.

But is not Vimalakīrti's reply also dualistic? Speech and silence are opposites. To explain the Bodhisattva's entry into non-duality in terms of silence is therefore surely as dualistic as explaining it in terms of speech. What is the entry into non-duality here? The answer is that Vimalakīrti does not have a concept of silence. He acts spontaneously according to the circumstances. That is why his silence here is meaningful. After all, there is silence and silence. In chapters 3 and 4 the Arhants and Bodhisattvas were reduced to silence when they encountered Vimalakīrti. In chapter 8 Śāriputra was reduced to silence by the goddess. But theirs was the silence of stupefaction. Vimalakīrti's is the silence of understanding, the silence of Enlightenment.

Vimalakīrti uses silence, but he has no concept of using it. He uses it as a means to an end, to communicate, but he also uses speech whenever necessary. He does not stick to silence. In fact, in the course of the *Vimalakīrti-nirdeśa* he says rather a lot. And speech and silence are not his only means of communication. He communicates also through marvellous magical displays. The means of communication are, in fact, infinite, as we shall see in the next chapter.

7

The Mystery of Human Communication

What can possibly follow Vimalakīrti's thunder-like silence? One might think that almost anything, however sublime, however impressive, would be an anti-climax. But as it turns out, it is not really so difficult to follow – not, at least, for Śāriputra. At the beginning of chapter 10 we find him worrying again. The text says:

> 'Thereupon, the venerable Śāriputra thought to himself, "If these great bodhisattvas do not adjourn before noontime, when are they going to eat?"'[61]

A short while ago, he was worrying about chairs. Now he is worrying about lunch.

But why is he so concerned that they should eat before noon? Well, Śāriputra is a monk, and according to the Hīnayāna *Vinaya*, the monastic law, monks are supposed to finish eating by noon. If they haven't managed to have a meal by then, they just have to wait until the following morning. Even then, they are not permitted to eat until they can clearly distinguish the lines on their own hand by means of natural light.

This rule is still observed in many parts of the Buddhist world. I followed it myself for several years when I lived in India, and there is quite a lot I could say about what some monks used rather irreverently to call 'the twelve o'clock business'. Monks are generally dependent for food on the laity. I often noticed that if lunch had not made its appearance by 11.30am – or even 10.30 – some of my fellow monks became very uneasy. A few started worrying about lunch as soon as breakfast was over. And some would get up at the crack of dawn so that they could have an enormous breakfast, then go back to bed and have a second breakfast later, and still have time for lunch before twelve o'clock. In a famous passage Buddhaghoṣa declares that someone is a 'one-mealer' even if they eat ten meals, provided they eat them all before noon. This is the Theravāda at its most ridiculously formalistic.

What I do take seriously is the principle of moderation in eating – and you could practise this by eating only in the evening as effectively as by eating only in the morning. The Sufis apparently try to observe a perpetual Ramadan, eating only after dark. But you could eat ten times a day and still be practising moderate eating, if you ate just a small quantity. The important thing is to eat mindfully, and eat only what is really necessary for health and strength.

It is a good thing to have a definite framework of behaviour, definite guidelines, especially when one is young, and it is even a good thing to be quite strict in observing those guidelines. An old brahmin lawyer I used to know in India, a very rigid, orthodox old man, was fond of saying 'A disciplined life gives strength,' and this is true. In the case of this old man, he derived his strength from following the brahminical rules, with some of which I would violently disagree because they involved the strict observance of the caste system. But they did make him into a very strong character, because he believed that he was following a divinely inspired way of life.

But following a system of discipline doesn't necessarily have any spiritual value at all. You develop a kind of strength in the army, in which you are governed by a certain ethos and have to observe certain rules. And even the 'rules' of Buddhism, the guidelines which you find in the traditional Vinaya-Piṭaka, are not necessarily helpful to us now. The principle behind all of them is probably still valid, but it may require a different application, a different expression. It might be a useful exercise to go through all the Vinaya rules systematically, examining each rule to see what principle is involved, how it was applied or formulated in the Buddha's day, whether that formulation still applies, and, if not, what fresh formulation of that principle might be helpful.

Some Theravādins would argue that one should continue to observe the rules out of faith in the Buddha. This sort of attitude cannot be disregarded altogether, but one could argue that it could not be the result of faith, because the Buddha encouraged his followers to think for themselves. The value of observing rules is not to be underestimated, but one has to give careful thought to what rules one does observe and why; one should not be inflexible about it.

It is no good trying to defend the Vinaya rules by saying 'If it was good enough for the Buddha, it's good enough for me.' We shouldn't just accept the tradition unthinkingly. It's a question of finding a middle way. You can't go it alone, relying in a one-sided, individualistic way on your own judgement, your own opinion; you need to consult with those who are wiser and more experienced than yourself. On the other hand, you don't want to submit unquestioningly to authority. It is not easy to follow this middle path, but we have to try. There has to be a place for faith and there has to be a place for healthy scepticism. It is very easy to go from one extreme to the other, rather than searching for the middle way. But if we are going to accept some authority unquestioningly, why bother with Buddhism? Why not just go and join the Catholic Church, which is so much closer to us in culture? Why give ourselves the trouble of going to the East and setting up an infallible authority there? And on the other hand, if you're going to be a thoroughgoing sceptic, why bother with Buddhism at all? Go and be a humanist, go and be an agnostic. Buddhism is a middle way between the extreme of authoritarianism and the extreme of individualistic thinking for oneself.

Whether or not Śāriputra is going to extremes, here we find him getting sidetracked once again. And once again Vimalakīrti takes him to task. He knows what Śāriputra is thinking, of course, and he says

> 'Reverend Śāriputra, the Tathāgata has taught the eight liberations. You should concentrate on those liberations, listening to the Dharma with a mind free of preoccupations with material things. Just wait a minute, reverend Śāriputra, and you will eat such food as you have never before tasted.'

Vimalakīrti then puts himself into a state of deep concentration and exerts his magical power. As a result, the whole assembly is enabled to see a far distant Buddha-land. There are, as we have seen, an infinite number of Buddha-lands or Pure Lands, each with its own characteristics. And here, in chapter 10, 'The Feast Brought by the Emanated Incarnation', we find ourselves introduced to another one. Like so many places and people in the Buddhist scriptures, it has rather a long name – Sarvagaṇḍha-sugaṇḍhā, which means 'Sweetly Fragrant with All Fragrances' or

'Sweetly Perfumed with All Perfumes' – and it is to be found in the zenith, the upward direction, infinitely distant from our own wretched, impure Buddha-land. The text says that it is 'beyond as many buddha-fields as there are sands in forty-two Ganges rivers.' That kind of distance takes quite a bit of imagining.

This Buddha-land is presided over by the Buddha Sugaṇḍhakuṭā, which means 'Heap of Fragrance' or 'Mountain of Perfume'. The trees emit a wonderful fragrance, which, we are told, 'far surpasses all the fragrances, human and divine, of all the buddha-fields of the ten directions'. Even the names of Arhant and Pratyeka-buddha are unheard of here. The Buddha Sugaṇḍhakuṭā teaches the Dharma to an assembly consisting exclusively of Bodhisattvas. All the houses, the avenues, the parks, and the palaces are made not of brick and stone, not of marble, not even of jewels, as they often are in the Mahāyāna sūtras, but of perfume. And the fragrance of the food eaten by the Bodhisattvas in that Pure Land pervades and permeates innumerable universes.

So, through Vimalakīrti's magical power, the whole assembly is enabled to 'see' – or rather experience – this Pure Land Sarvagaṇḍha-sugaṇḍhā, which consists entirely of perfumes. And just at the moment that it is revealed to them, the Buddha Sugaṇḍhakuṭā and his Bodhisattvas sit down to a meal. (Apparently it is lunch-time there too.) The meal is served by a class of deities called Gaṇḍhabyūhāhāra ('Gloriously Perfumed'), all of whom are devoted to the Mahāyāna.

Vimalakīrti asks the assembly gathered in his invisible house if anyone would like to go to that Buddha-land and bring back some food. But, rather strangely, nobody is willing to go. The reason is that they have all been restrained from offering to make the journey by the supernatural power of Mañjuśrī, the Bodhisattva of Wisdom. Luk's translation here is 'All the Bodhisattvas remained silent as Mañjuśrī was noted for his supernatural power,' while according to Thurman no one volunteered because they were restrained by Mañjuśrī's magical power, and Lamotte says 'Through the supernatural intervention (*adhiṣṭhāna*) of Mañjuśrī ... all the Bodhisattvas kept silent.' It seems quite clear that the original must be 'because of Mañjuśrī's supernatural power'. One translator takes that to mean that Mañjuśrī actually intervened with his supernatural power, while the other interprets it that Mañjuśrī had the reputation of possessing such power. Incidentally, Lamotte's assertion that Mañjuśrī's supernatural intervention, as he renders it, is equivalent to *adhiṣṭhāna* is not quite right; it's more like the Sanskrit *ṛddhi*, supernatural power.

The point here is that Mañjuśrī wants to give Vimalakīrti an opportunity to show what he is capable of. He doesn't want the other Bodhisattvas present to make an exhibition of their own blundering efforts to go to this other Buddha-land, so he prevents them from volunteering so that they can see what Vimalakīrti can do. This seems to me to be the sense of the text. If Mañjuśrī is 'restraining' the Bodhisattvas in some way, it can only be as a skilful means; it cannot be for any selfish motive.

Vimalakīrti obligingly takes this opportunity to perform a magical feat. By means of his magical power, he emanates an incarnation Bodhisattva of youthful appearance, adorned with all sorts of auspicious marks and signs, and so beautiful that he outshines the whole assembly. Vimalakīrti directs the emanated incarnation to go to the Pure Land 'Sweetly Perfumed with All Perfumes', bow down before the Buddha Sugaṇḍhakuṭā, and say that Vimalakīrti asks for the remains of his meal, because with those remains Vimalakīrti 'will accomplish the Buddha-work in the universe called Sahā'. Sahā ('Suffering' or 'Tribulation') is, of course, our own world.

And so the emanated incarnation goes to that distant Buddha-land, is given the food in a perfumed vessel, and, in a fraction of a second, returns with it to Vimalakīrti. And that is not all he returns with. He is accompanied by ninety million Bodhisattvas, who have been given leave to come by Sugaṇḍhakuṭā. Vimalakīrti, of course, makes room for all of them in his house. This time he doesn't bother bringing in more thrones from elsewhere; he just creates them out of thin air.

The fragrance of the food brought back spreads throughout the entire great city of Vaiśālī and beyond – spreads, in fact, throughout a hundred universes. Noticing the fragrance of this wonderful perfume, everybody in Vaiśālī is amazed, and filled with joy and elation. They feel purified by the perfume, cleansed in body and mind. And they all come flocking to Vimalakīrti's house, where they too sit down, all eighty-four thousand of them. The gods too, we are told, are attracted by the perfume, and they also turn up at Vimalakīrti's house. And everybody in this now truly vast assembly is then given a portion of the food to eat.

As he distributes the food, Vimalakīrti says:

> 'Reverends, eat of the food of the Tathāgata! It is ambrosia perfumed by the great compassion. But do not fix your minds in narrow-minded attitudes, lest you be unable to receive its gift.'[62]

Once everyone has been fed – so many tens of millions of beings – there is just as much food as before. And having eaten, everybody present is completely satisfied. They all experience a deep spiritual bliss, and a wonderful perfume emanates from the pores of their skin.

Vimalakīrti then asks the Bodhisattvas who have recently arrived how the Buddha Sugaṇḍhakuṭā teaches his Dharma. They tell him:

> 'The Tathāgata [the Buddha of that Buddha-land] 'does not teach the Dharma by means of sound and language. He disciplines the bodhisattvas only by means of perfumes. At the foot of each perfume-tree sits a bodhisattva, and the trees emit perfumes like this one. From the moment they smell that perfume, the bodhisattvas attain the concentration called "source of all bodhisattva-virtues". From the moment they attain that concentration, all the Bodhisattva-virtues are produced in them.'

The Bodhisattvas then return Vimalakīrti's question, asking him how the Buddha Śākyamuni, 'our' Buddha, teaches the Dharma in our world. And Vimalakīrti replies:

> 'Good sirs, these living beings here are hard to discipline. Therefore, he teaches them with discourses appropriate for the disciplining of the wild and uncivilized. How does he discipline the wild and uncivilized? What discourses are appropriate? Here they are:
>
> '"This is hell. This is the animal world. This is the world of the lord of death. These are the adversities. These are the rebirths with crippled faculties. These are physical misdeeds, and these are the retributions for physical misdeeds. These are verbal misdeeds, and these are the retributions for verbal misdeeds. These are mental misdeeds, and these are the retributions for mental misdeeds. This is killing. This is stealing. This is sexual misconduct. This is lying. This is backbiting. This is harsh speech. This is frivolous speech. This is covetousness. This is malice. This is false view. These are their retributions. This is miserliness, and this is its effect. This is immorality. This is hatred. This is sloth. This is the fruit of sloth. This is false wisdom and this is the fruit of false wisdom. These are the transgressions of the precepts. This is the vow of personal liberation. This should be done and that should not be done. This is proper and that should be abandoned. This is an obscuration and that is without obscuration. This is sin and that rises above sin. This is the path and that is the wrong path. This is virtue and that is evil. This is blameworthy and that is blameless. This is defiled and that is immaculate. This is mundane and that is transcendental. This is compounded and that is uncompounded. This is passion and that is

purification. This is life and that is liberation."

'Thus, by means of these varied explanations of the Dharma, the Buddha trains the minds of those living beings who are just like wild horses. Just as wild horses or wild elephants will not be tamed unless the goad pierces them to the marrow, so living beings who are wild and hard to civilize are disciplined only by means of discourses about all kinds of miseries.'[63]

Most of this is straightforward, not to say blunt. There is just one aspect of it that may require a little explanation. Vimalakīrti says that the Buddha teaches that 'this is false wisdom and this is the fruit of false wisdom'. 'False wisdom' is a very misleading translation, making it sound as though there are two kinds of wisdom, one true and one false. The Sanskrit word here is *dausprajñā*, and this corresponds to the Pali *dupañña*, a term which occurs several times in the *Dhammapada*, and is usually translated 'evil understanding'. One could say that *dupañña* and *micchādiṭṭhi*, 'false view', are roughly synonymous, but that *micchādiṭṭhi* is a much more precise technical term. A *micchādiṭṭhi* is a certain definite point of view which is wrong. *Dupañña* is just the general state of having an evil or wrong understanding, an understanding clouded by unskilful mental factors. One could say that *micchādiṭṭhi* is *dupañña* articulated into specific philosophical positions which are mistaken. So *prajñā* is being used here in its more general sense of 'understanding'. *Prajñā* in the highest sense could not possibly be false.

Conditions in this very impure Buddha-land are such, Vimalakīrti says, that Bodhisattvas who work here have to have very strong compassion and determination – much stronger, in fact, than that of Bodhisattvas in Buddha-lands such as Sarvagaṇḍhasugaṇḍhā. Such Bodhisattvas accomplish, therefore, correspondingly greater benefits for living beings. Then, after a few more exchanges between the visiting Bodhisattvas and Vimalakīrti about the practices and qualities that a Bodhisattva in this Buddha-land needs, the chapter ends.

There is a great deal that could be said about all these incidents and the figures involved in them. By this I do not mean that there are a lot of specific points that could be made in the ordinary discursive way. It is more that if you allow your mind to dwell upon this particular episode, a number of different facets and aspects of its significance disclose themselves. You could investigate, for instance, why the emanation Bodhisattva bows down when he arrives in that other Pure Land. Why does Vimalakīrti ask for the remains of the meal, and why does Sugaṇḍhakuṭā comply with his request? What does the meal itself signify? What does the ambrosia or *amṛta*, the nectar of immortality of which the food consists, represent? Is there some meaningful connection to be made between the vessel in which the food is contained and the Holy Grail? And why is the food it contains not depleted, even though millions of beings have been fed? There is plenty of scope for imaginative reflection here.

We will focus, however, on just one topic. We have heard that the Tathāgata Sugaṇḍhakuṭā teaches his Dharma, 'disciplines' the Bodhisattvas, not through sound and language but through perfumes. Perfumes are his medium of communication. This may seem to us very bizarre, but what a nice way of being disciplined!

Like the other physical senses, the sense-consciousness of smell arises through the contact of sense-organ and sense-object. But in the case of the sense of smell, rather curiously, there is less direct contact between the two than there is between the eye and shapes and colours, or the ear and sounds. In the case of the sense of smell there is a kind of intermediary. A rose in a distant garden emits millions of tiny invisible particles; some of them enter our nostrils and come into contact with the olfactory nerve endings; and we 'smell' the rose.

Scent, or perfume, is an extremely subtle thing. We can't see it, we can't hear it, but it is very definitely there. Almost everybody can distinguish a 'good' smell from a 'bad' smell, a perfume from a stink, but smell very often affects us on an almost unconscious level and can therefore be used to create a mood or feeling. This has led to the manufacture of all sorts of artificial odours which are used in various ways. They are used in social life, when we want to make ourselves more attractive – or at least less offensive – to other people. They are also used in religious life to create a particular kind of atmosphere – many religions, for example, use particular kinds of incense in connection with certain ceremonies and observances – which suggests a definite connection between certain odours and certain mental and emotional states.

The sense of smell is the least well developed of all our senses. In this respect we are very different from certain other animals. In dogs, for instance, the sense of smell is very highly developed, more so indeed than their other senses. It is said that dogs experience, and therefore live in, quite a different world from human beings: a world of odours. When the dog puts its nose outside the door, it experiences hundreds of different smells coming from all directions, all quite vivid and distinct one from another, and all meaning something. Some human beings, of course, have a more acute sense of smell than others, but certainly not as acute as that of dogs and other animals.

Perfume can therefore be said to be a symbol for something very subtle and delicate; something that is quite intangible, yet definitely there; something that can be perceived and that can have certain effects on us, even from a distance. According to the Mahāyāna, the subtlest of all influences is the influence of the Buddhas and Bodhisattvas, the influence of Enlightenment, the influence of great Compassion. It is not easily perceived, yet in a sense it is always present, like radio waves in the air. Great Compassion is not just an individual emotion, at however high a level. It is a transcendental emanation of Reality itself, of the Reality with which the Buddhas and great Bodhisattvas are at one. In the mythic language of the *Vimalakīrti-nirdeśa*, this Reality is *amṛta*, which literally means 'deathless'. It is what the Greeks called ambrosia, the nectar of immortality. And this ambrosia is perfumed. Vimalakīrti says to Śāriputra and the great disciples:

> 'Reverends, eat of the food of the Tathāgata! It is ambrosia perfumed by the great compassion.'

In the Pure Land 'Sweetly Perfumed with all Perfumes' Sugaṇḍhakuṭā and the Bodhisattvas regularly feast on this ambrosia. They feast on Reality, they are nourished by it, and they are therefore pervaded by its influence, by the perfume of compassion. In fact, the whole of that Pure Land is pervaded by it. Everything there is made of it, made of Compassion. 'In that universe, all the houses, the avenues, the parks, and the palaces are made of various perfumes.' It is a universe of purely spiritual, purely transcendental influences. Power in the sense of force does not exist there, in however subtle a form. In this way we may descry something of the meaning of what is going on when Vimalakīrti has the ambrosia brought from Sugaṇḍhakuṭā's Pure Land, when its fragrance pervades the entire great city of Vaiśālī, and when it permeates and pervades one hundred universes. And we can begin to see the nature of its effect on the people of Vaiśālī and the gods and goddesses.

We find this same symbolism in an important and historically influential text of Far Eastern Buddhism: *The Awakening of Faith in the Mahāyāna*. Mahāyāna here refers not just to a particular form of Buddhism; it means something like 'Great Principle'. This work is not a sūtra – it is not represented as being a discourse by the Buddha – but a *śāstra*, a text attributed to a great Buddhist teacher, in this case Aśvaghoṣa. It survives only in Chinese translation, and according to some scholars it was actually composed in China. It speaks of ultimate Reality as *tathatā* or *bhūta-tathatā*. *Tathatā* means simply 'suchness'. *Bhuṭa-tathatā* means 'the suchness of things'. Ultimate Reality is 'such as it is'; it can't be described. If you ask what Reality is, the only possible answer is that it is 'such as it is'. All that you can say about Reality is that it is characterized by 'suchness' or 'such-as-it-is-ness'.

This ultimate Reality is spoken of in *The Awakening of Faith in the Mahāyāna* as 'perfuming' conditioned existence. Something of Reality 'rubs off', so to speak, on to conditioned existence. A few infinitesimally tiny 'particles' are 'transmitted', and we can therefore perceive ultimate Reality, however faintly, in the midst of conditioned existence. And, perceiving it, we can strive towards it.

Not only does Ultimate Reality 'perfume' conditioned existence. According to *The Awakening of Faith in the Mahāyāna*, conditioned existence 'perfumes' (if that is the right word) Ultimate Reality. And Ultimate Reality's response is to manifest Compassion. This is a very profound conception – but it gives us some idea of the appropriateness of perfume as a symbol for great Compassion, whose influence is so very subtle and delicate.

Practising meditation gives one at least a limited sense of this kind of influence. A time comes when you begin to sense something which you cannot describe or define. It doesn't come under any mundane category, yet at the same time there is nothing vague or cloudy about it. It is intensely vivid, intensely real, like the perfume of some unknown flower. We might say that it is the perfume of the thousand-petalled lotus itself, the lotus that blooms in the Pure Land.

Two things follow from the fact that we can have this kind of experience. First, just as we can perceive odours only because we have a sense of smell and a nose, in the same way we can perceive the subtle perfume of Ultimate Reality only because we have within us a kind of transcendental sense, something that has an affinity with the transcendental, something to which the 'particles' of the transcendental can be transmitted. This is what the Mahāyāna in a general way calls the *tathāgata-dhātu*, the element of Buddhahood. Secondly, this transcendental sense of ours can be developed, can be made more sensitive and more refined, to the extent that eventually it can tell us where the perfume is coming from and which direction we have to take to find its source.

We have seen that in the Buddha-land called 'Sweetly Perfumed with all Perfumes'. Sugaṇḍhakuṭā communicates the Dharma by means of perfume. This is not really such a strange idea as it may at first seem. In fact, we know from our own experience that perfume or odour is a means of communication. Everything and every place has its own distinctive odour. When I visited New Zealand, for example, I noticed the distinctive spicy smell of the countryside, the 'bush': very sweet, yet at the same time sharp and refreshing, even stimulating – and very different from anything that one can experience in England.

People also have an odour. Here we begin to tread on rather delicate ground – this is something that we are not supposed to talk about. A person's odour is not just due to hygiene and cosmetics. It is affected, for instance, by the type of food you eat. A vegetarian smells quite different from a meat-eater. My vegetarian friends in India say that sometimes they cannot bear being too near Westerners because of the smell – the smell, they believe, of the meat they have eaten.

Women smell different from men; children smell different from adults; and very young people smell different from very old people. People who come from one part of the world smell different from people who come from another. Dogs can recognize these distinctive natural odours, but most humans cannot – although they can certainly develop the capacity, and some so-called 'primitive' peoples have it, at least to some extent. It seems quite likely that all human beings originally had this power, but most of us have subsequently lost it, especially once we started living in settled communities, away from such close contact with nature. But one smell which many people can still recognize is what we might call the smell of death. When someone is dying of illness or old age, they give off a distinctive smell which can be perceived even by people whose sense of smell has been blunted by civilized living.

Smell has its part to play in communication. The most important factor in any communication is the emotional state of the people engaged in it; and emotional states produce all sorts of physical reactions, including glandular secretions which each have their own odour. We speak, for instance, of 'the smell of fear' or 'the smell of anxiety'. We do not often have occasion to speak about the odours of more positive emotions, probably because they are less powerfully and pungently developed. It is, however, well known that a perfume similar to that of roses or jasmine is sometimes perceived in a room where someone is meditating – not only by the meditator, but also by other people present.

Whether or not we are conscious of it, smell is very much part of our response to other people. So, although we tend to assume that communication is possible only through words, we should not really be surprised to learn that in the Buddha-land of Sugaṇḍhakuṭā, perfume is the means of communicating the Dharma. Of course, we may object that rarefied communication by perfume is all very well between Buddhas and Bodhisattvas at a transcendental level, but has little relevance to what goes on between ordinary human beings. But Buddhas and Bodhisattvas are human beings too. They may be Enlightened or partially Enlightened, but their communication, however rarefied, is still a form of human communication, and as such it can be developed by us too.

The important point is that words and language are not the only medium of communication; many others are possible. We find this emphasized in the next chapter of the *Vimalakīrti-nirdeśa*, chapter 11, which is called 'Lesson of the Destructible and the Indestructible'. At the beginning of this chapter there is a change of scene. We are no longer in the vast throne-filled mansion that Vimalakīrti's house has by now become, but back in Āmrapālī's Park with the Buddha, who is teaching the Dharma to the rest of the assembly. And as he teaches, the park becomes larger and larger. Not only that; the entire assembly is suffused with a beautiful golden light.

Ānanda is rather surprised by this, and asks the Buddha what it may mean. The Buddha replies that it means that Vimalakīrti and Mañjuśrī are on their way with a great multitude – and a few seconds later they all arrive. In fact, Vimalakīrti magically transports the entire assembly, thrones and all, on the palm of his right hand. When they have arrived, saluted the Buddha, and taken their thrones, Ānanda remarks on the strong scent of perfume which suddenly pervades the air. The Buddha tells him that it is emanating from the pores of all the Bodhisattvas. Śāriputra hastens to add that it is emanating from the pores of the Arhants too – and he explains to Ānanda how it has come about. After exchanging a few remarks with Vimalakīrti about the perfume and the food, and about how the perfume emanates from the bodies of all who have partaken of this food, Ānanda then says to the Buddha

> 'Lord, it is wonderful that this food accomplishes the work of the Buddha!'

And, in a very important passage, the Buddha replies:

> 'So it is, Ānanda! It is as you say, Ānanda! There are buddha-fields that accomplish the buddha-work by means of bodhisattvas; those that do so by means of lights; those that do so by means of the tree of enlightenment; those that do so by means of the physical beauty and the marks of the Tathāgata; those that do so by means of religious robes; those that do so by means of food; those that do so by means

> of water; those that do so by means of gardens; those that do so by means of palaces; those that do so by means of mansions; those that do so by means of magical incarnations; those that do so by means of empty space; those that do so by means of lights in the sky. Why is it so, Ānanda? Because by these various means, living beings become disciplined. Similarly, Ānanda, there are buddha-fields that accomplish the buddha-work by means of teaching living beings words, definitions, and examples, such as "dreams", "images", the "reflection of the moon in water", "echoes", "illusions", and "mirages"; and those that accomplish the buddha-work by making words understandable. Also, Ānanda, there are utterly pure buddha-fields that accomplish the buddha-work for living beings without speech, by silence, inexpressibility, and unteachability. Ānanda, among all the activities, enjoyments, and practices of the Buddhas, there are none that do not accomplish the buddha-work, because all discipline living beings. Finally, Ānanda, the Buddhas accomplish the buddha-work by means of the four Māras and all the eighty-four thousand types of passion that afflict living beings.'[64]

In this passage the Buddha goes much further than we have gone so far. He says that there are *many* alternative means of communication, many means to 'accomplish the buddha-work', to teach the Dharma. It is possible, he says, to communicate by means of Bodhisattvas – perhaps Vimalakīrti did this when he sent the golden emanation Bodhisattva to visit Sugaṇḍhakuṭā. Vimalakīrti has also communicated by various other means: through the food that was brought back, and through silence. It is also possible, the Buddha says, to communicate by means of the Bodhi tree. This makes me think of examples of early Indian Buddhist art which do not represent the human figure of the Buddha, but just show the Bodhi tree as a symbol of the Buddha's presence. And there is even the possibility, apparently, of communicating by means of 'lights in the sky'. Naturally, some people will take this to be a reference to UFOs, which are said to be an attempt on the part of extra-terrestrial beings to communicate with people on earth.

Be that as it may, we do need to be reminded of these alternative means of communication, because we tend to depend too much on words and language. (This tendency is perhaps not quite so pronounced in Asia and Africa as it is in the West.) Only too often we feel that we have not really expressed ourselves unless we have put it all into words, unless we have spelled everything out in full verbal detail. Educated people are particularly prone to this. Of course, we have already seen how important it is for the Bodhisattva to express himself clearly and correctly: we need to be articulate. But we should not think that when we have put something into words, whatever it is has necessarily been fully expressed. There are alternative ways of communicating.

In fact, we do not rely entirely on words, even though we may think we do. When you compare a written transcription of a seminar with a tape-recording, for example, the written version seems to have a dimension missing. Listening to the tape, you hear not only the words but also the way in which they were used – the tone, the pace, the pitch, the volume – all of which contribute to what the speakers wanted to say. If the seminar was video-taped, you would get an even better impression of what the participants wanted to communicate, because you would have not only words and sounds, but also gestures, expressions, and so on. In the Buddhist scriptures, of course, we have only the words of the Buddha. Something of the context is often given, but we do not have his tone of voice or the look with which he said something. We do not have the Buddha himself saying it. We have only the words – and this surely makes a big difference.

In exploring 'alternative' means of communication, we are not simply seeking to exchange one means for another. Different means of communication allow us to communicate different things. It has been said that when we learn a new language, we acquire a new soul. It is certainly true that we can say things that we could not say before, as I know from my own experience. There are some things that I can say in Hindi that I can't say in English. The words may be translatable, but somehow they fail to convey the entire meaning, all the nuances and connotations. And some languages are more suitable for certain purposes than others. When asked what language he usually spoke, Charles V, the Holy Roman Emperor in the sixteenth century, replied that when he spoke with his courtiers, he spoke in French; when he spoke to his mistress, he spoke in Italian; when he spoke to God – that is, when he said his prayers – he spoke in Spanish; and when he spoke to his horse, he spoke in German.

The same applies to alternative means of communication. With them we can say things that we could not say before. It is not simply that they enable us to say the same things in a different way; with them we can say different things. It's like having an additional sense through which more of the universe is revealed. It is well known that our physical perceptions are very limited: the eye perceives only a certain spectrum of colours; the ear perceives only a narrow range of sounds; and the nose perceives only a very few odours. The same applies to our mental perceptions, the perceptions of our ordinary conscious mind. They too are very limited, and in any case they function entirely within the distorting overall framework of the subject–object relationship.

It is important, therefore, that we acquire new senses and new means of communication. The more means of communication we have at our disposal, the better. So let us learn to communicate in terms of perfumes. Let us learn to communicate in terms of silence. Let us learn to communicate in terms of 'lights in the sky'. It is important that we very much enlarge the total range of our being and consciousness. The mystery of human communication is perhaps even greater than we had supposed.

8

The Four Great Reliances: Criteria for the Spiritual Life

Throughout north-eastern India, where the Buddha lived and taught, there are scattered a number of places which have special associations with events in the Buddha's life. There is Bodh-gaya, where he gained Enlightenment; Sarnath, where he first taught the Dharma; Śrāvasti, where he spent many rainy seasons and gave many teachings; and Kuśinagara, where he finally passed away between the twin sal trees.

All these holy places have their own atmospheres, and their own ways of commemorating the Buddha. But although they are so different, the sacred sites have one thing in common: they all have stūpas. A stūpa is a reliquary, a dome-shaped structure which contains – or supposedly contains – a body relic of the Buddha or one of his disciples: a tiny fragment of bone or ash. The Indian ones are made of brick faced with stone, and they are often quite enormous.[65]

In the course of the centuries the stūpas at the sacred sites have been neglected, and some have even been plundered for their materials. As late as the eighteenth century, for instance, bricks were taken from one of the great stūpas at Sarnath to build a market-place in the city of Varanasi. Today many of the stūpas are little more than heaps of rubble. But even those that are relatively undamaged, or have been restored to some extent, have a desolate, uncared-for look. After all, the Archaeological Department's responsibility is just to restore them – not to decorate them or make them beautiful. It is true that among the many tourists and sightseers, increasing number of pilgrims now visit the major sites. Even so, these places are a sad and feeble shadow of what they were one or two thousand years ago.

In those days, all the stūpas would have been intact, and they would have been entirely covered with stone, much of it elaborately carved. Moreover, each stūpa would have been beautifully decorated with multitudes of coloured flags and banners, and all sorts of streamers, some of them made of gold or silver plates hinged together, just as one sees in Nepal even today. Each stūpa would have been hung with strings of pearls and festoons of flowers. At night one would have seen hundreds of tiny oil lamps burning in all the niches. And on the four sides of the stūpa – north, south, east, and west – gateways of sweet-smelling Indian flowers would have been set up.

Above all, around the stūpas there would have been thousands upon thousands of pilgrims, all dressed in garments of spotless white. They would not have been aimlessly milling around, gaping at the stūpa like tourists. They would have been circumambulating it: walking round and round it, keeping it on their right as a sign of respect. They would have processed around it, perhaps eight or ten abreast, carrying in their hands trays containing all sorts of offerings: flowers, lights and lamps, sticks of lighted incense. And as they marched round and round, they would have chanted the Refuges and Precepts, and all sorts of devotional verses in praise of the Buddha and the great Bodhisattvas. Accompanying the chanting there would have been the sound of drums and other musical instruments. Altogether it must have been a truly wonderful spectacle, especially when the sun shone down on it all from a clear blue sky.

This sort of observance, which was very popular with Buddhists in ancient India, is usually known as 'stūpa worship'. But this is not quite correct. The devotees were not really worshipping the structure of brick and stone, however beautiful it was. They were worshipping the body relics of the Buddha, enshrined within the stūpa, and thus worshipping the Buddha. This sort of worship, known as *amisa-pūja* or 'worship with material things', has, of course, its counterpart – with greater or lesser degrees of splendour – in all religious traditions.

But in chapter 13 of the *Vimalakīrti-nirdeśa* – which, together with chapter 14, Thurman entitles simply 'Epilogue' – a fundamental question arises. Is there not a better way of worshipping the Buddha? It is in the course of the answer to this question that we come across the four great reliances as criteria for the spiritual life. But although it is in chapter 13 that this question is asked directly, we get some hint of it in the previous chapter: 'Vision of the Universe of Abhirati and the Tathāgata Akṣobhya'.

The vision of the title is the main event of the chapter, and it comes about when Śāriputra asks the Buddha in which Buddha-land Vimalakīrti died before being reborn in this, our world. The Buddha tells Śāriputra to ask Vimalakīrti himself – but Vimalakīrti, perhaps predictably, is rather unhelpful, becoming very metaphysical and paradoxical. So the Buddha comes to Śāriputra's rescue. He says that Vimalakīrti comes from the presence of the Buddha Akṣobhya in the universe Abhirati, and has been reborn in this Sahā universe, this universe of suffering and tribulation, not as a result of his past karma, but voluntarily. He has come here to purify living beings and to make the light of wisdom shine in the midst of the darkness of the passions. Having heard this, everybody present in the great assembly wants to see Abhirati; so Vimalakīrti, at the Buddha's request, shows it to them by means of his magical power.

The hint we are looking for – as to a better way of worshipping the Buddha – comes in a little exchange between the Buddha and Vimalakīrti at the beginning of the chapter. The Buddha asks Vimalakīrti

> 'Noble son, when you would see the Tathāgata [the Buddha], how do you view him?'

And Vimalakīrti replies:

> 'Lord, when I would see the Tathāgata, I view him by not seeing any Tathāgata. Why? I see him as not born from the past, not passing on to the future, and not abiding in the present time. Why? He is the essence which is the reality of matter, but he is not matter. He is the essence which is the reality of sensation, but he is not sensation. He is the essence which is the reality of intellect, but he is not intellect. He is the essence which is the reality of motivation, yet he is not motivation. He is the essence which is the reality of consciousness, yet he is not consciousness. Like the element of space, he does not abide in any of the four elements. Transcending the scope of eye, ear, nose, tongue, body, and mind, he is not produced in the six sense-media. He is not involved in the three worlds, is free of the three defilements, is associated with the triple liberation, is endowed with the three knowledges, and has truly attained the unattainable.
>
> 'The Tathāgata has reached the extreme of detachment in regard to

all things, yet he is not a reality-limit. He abides in ultimate reality, yet there is no relationship between it and him. He is not produced from causes, nor does he depend on conditions. He is not without any characteristic, nor has he any characteristic. He has no single nature nor any diversity of natures. He is not a conception, not a mental construction, nor is he a nonconception. He is neither the other shore, nor this shore, nor that between. He is neither here, nor there, nor anywhere else. He is neither this nor that. He cannot be discovered by consciousness, nor is he inherent in consciousness. He is neither darkness nor light. He is neither name nor sign. He is neither weak nor strong. He lives in no country or direction. He is neither good nor evil. He is neither compounded nor uncompounded. He cannot be explained as having any meaning whatsoever.

'The Tathāgata is neither generosity nor avarice, neither morality nor immorality, neither tolerance nor malice, neither effort nor sloth, neither concentration nor distraction, neither wisdom nor foolishness. He is inexpressible. He is neither truth nor falsehood; neither escape from the world nor failure to escape from the world; neither cause of involvement in the world nor not a cause of involvement in the world; he is the cessation of all theory and all practice. He is neither a field of merit nor not a field of merit; he is neither worthy of offerings nor unworthy of offerings. He is not an object, and cannot be contacted. He is not a whole, nor a conglomeration. He surpasses all calculations. He is utterly unequaled, yet equal to the ultimate reality of things. He is matchless, especially in effort. He surpasses all measure. He does not go, does not stay, does not pass beyond. He is neither seen, heard, distinguished, nor known. He is without any complexity, having attained the equanimity of omniscient gnosis. Equal towards all things, he does not discriminate between them. He is without reproach, without excess, without corruption, without conception, and without intellectualization. He is without activity, without birth, without occurrence, without origin, without production, and without nonproduction. He is without fear and without subconsciousness; without sorrow, without joy, and without strain. No verbal teaching can express him.

'Such is the body of the Tathāgata and thus should he be seen. Who sees thus, truly sees. Who sees otherwise, sees falsely.'[66]

In other words, the Buddha is to be identified with his spiritual essence. He is to be identified with what makes him a Buddha: with his Enlightenment, with his realization of the nature of ultimate Reality. So worship of the Buddha must go far beyond the worship of his body relics enshrined in a stūpa. Not that stūpa worship is wrong – it helps to develop devotional feeling – but the body relics are not the Buddha. The Buddha, in fact, is not to be identified with his material body at all – not even during his lifetime.

So, if it is good to develop devotional feelings, but worship of body relics is not enough, what should be worshipped? This is the opening theme of the next chapter of the text, chapter 13. Here we are again concerned with the question of previous incarnations, including those of the Buddha Śākyamuni himself. At the beginning of the chapter we find Śakra, more usually known as Indra, the king of the gods, coming forward. He says that he has never before heard such a wonderful teaching as this *Vimalakīrti-nirdeśa* and he praises it at length. He also promises to protect it. (From all this, incidentally, we can gather that the text is beginning to come to an end.)

Approving of what Śakra says, the Buddha asks him to imagine that the whole great universe is full of Buddhas, as full of Buddhas as it is of plants, bushes, grass, and trees. Suppose, he says, these Buddhas passed away into *parinirvāṇa*, or – in ordinary parlance – suppose they died. And suppose somebody erected marvellous stūpas for each and every one of them, stūpas made entirely of precious stones, each stūpa as large as a world. Suppose that devotee spent a whole aeon or more worshipping all those stūpas with flowers, perfumes, and music. They would certainly gain much merit. But, the Buddha continues, if someone were to accept, recite, and understand deeply the exposition of Dharma called 'Instruction in the Inconceivable Emancipation', their merits would be far greater. Why? Because the Enlightenment of the Buddhas arises from the Dharma, so one truly honours the Buddhas not by material offerings, but by honouring the Dharma.

This may be clear enough, but how does one go about 'Dharma worship'? What is Dharma worship? The Buddha answers this question by way of further instruction to Śakra, in the course of which he refers to events of the remote past. Once upon a time, the Buddha says, (the text doesn't actually say 'once upon a time', but there is that sort of feeling to the story coming up) there was a Buddha called Bhaiṣajyarāja, 'King of Healing' or 'Medicine King'. He lived an inconceivably long time ago and his lifespan was twenty short aeons. He had a retinue of thirty-six million billion disciples, that is, followers of the Hīnayāna, and also a retinue of twelve million billion Bodhisattvas, or followers of the Mahāyāna. At the same time, there lived a universal monarch called Ratnacchattra, 'Precious Umbrella' or 'Precious Parasol', and he had a thousand sons. This king and his sons were very devoted to the Buddha Bhaiṣajyarāja. They all worshipped him by making many offerings of material things, and they continued to do so for ten whole aeons.

But there was one prince – the odd man out or, we might say, the individual – who was not satisfied with this sort of thing. We might even go so far as to say that he was fed up with it all. His name was Candracchattra, 'Lunar Umbrella' or 'Lunar Parasol'. Retiring into solitude, Candracchattra thought to himself 'Is there not another mode of worship, even better and more noble than this?' And he got an answer. The gods spoke to him from the sky, and they said 'Good man, the supreme worship is the Dharma-worship.' Whether or not Candracchattra was at all taken aback by this occurrence the text doesn't tell us, but he asked the gods what this 'Dharma-worship' might be, and they replied 'Go to the Tathāgata Bhaiṣajyarāja, and he will tell you.'

So Candracchattra duly went to see Bhaiṣajyarāja, and put to him the same question: 'What is Dharma-worship?' And Bhaiṣajyarāja replied:

> 'Noble son, the Dharma-worship is that worship rendered to the discourses taught by the Tathāgata. These discourses are deep and profound in illumination. They do not conform to the mundane and are difficult to understand and difficult to see and difficult to realize. They are subtle, precise, and ultimately incomprehensible. As Scriptures, they are collected in the canon of the bodhisattvas, stamped with the insignia of the king of incantations and teachings. They reveal the irreversible wheel of Dharma, arising from the six transcendences, cleansed of any false notions. They are endowed with all the aids to enlightenment and embody the seven factors of enlightenment. They introduce living beings to the great compassion and teach them the great love. They eliminate all the convictions of the Māras, and they manifest relativity.
>
> 'They contain the message of selflessness, living-beinglessness, lifelessness, personlessness, voidness, signlessness, wishlessness, nonperformance, nonproduction, and nonoccurrence.
>
> 'They make possible the attainment of the seat of enlightenment and set in motion the wheel of the Dharma. They are approved and praised by the chiefs of the gods, nāgas, yakṣas, gandharvas, āsuras, garuḍas, kiṁnaras, and mahoragas. They preserve unbroken the

heritage of the holy Dharma, contain the treasury of the Dharma, and represent the summit of the Dharma-worship. They are upheld by all holy beings and teach all the bodhisattva practices. They induce the unmistaken understanding of the Dharma in its ultimate sense. They certify that all things are impermanent, miserable, selfless, and peaceful, thus epitomizing the Dharma. They cause the abandonment of avarice, immorality, malice, laziness, forgetfulness, foolishness, and jealousy, as well as bad convictions, adherence to objects, and all opposition. They are praised by all the Buddhas. They are the medicines for the tendencies of mundane life, and they authentically manifest the great happiness of liberation. To teach correctly, to uphold, to investigate, and to understand such Scriptures, thus incorporating into one's own life the holy Dharma – that is the "Dharma-worship".

'Furthermore, noble son, the Dharma-worship consists of determining the Dharma according to the Dharma; applying the Dharma according to the Dharma; being in harmony with relativity; being free of extremist convictions; attaining the tolerance of ultimate birthlessness and nonoccurrence of all things; realizing selflessness and living-beinglessness; refraining from struggle about causes and conditions, without quarreling, or disputing; not being possessive; being free of egoism; relying on the meaning and not the literal expression; relying on gnosis and not on consciousness; relying on the ultimate teachings definitive in meaning and not insisting on the superficial teachings interpretable in meaning; relying on reality and not insisting on opinions derived from personal authorities; realizing correctly the reality of the Buddha; realizing the ultimate absence of any fundamental consciousness; and overcoming the habit of clinging to an ultimate ground. Finally, attaining peace by stopping everything from ignorance to old age, death, sorrow, lamentation, misery, anxiety, and trouble, and realizing that living beings know no end to their views concerning these twelve links of dependent origination; then, noble son, when you do not hold to any view at all, it is called the unexcelled Dharma-worship.'[67]

So this is Bhaiṣajyarāja's explanation of Dharma-worship – and when Candracchattra heard it, he was overwhelmed by a profound transcendental experience. Vowing to devote himself to the Dharma and to attain Supreme Enlightenment, without delay he went forth from home into the homeless life.

Having told the story, the Buddha proceeds to identify the characters in it for Śakra's benefit. He says that King Ratnacchattra was none other than the Buddha Ratnarcis, as he afterwards became, and his thousand sons are the thousand Bodhisattvas of the present aeon. And Prince Candracchattra was the Buddha Śākyamuni himself in a previous life.

So, as this story shows, there *is* a better way of worshipping the Buddha than by making offerings of material things, and it is known as Dharma-worship. And the first thing that Bhaiṣajyarāja mentions as constituting Dharma-worship is 'determining the Dharma according to the Dharma; applying the Dharma according to the Dharma' – or, as Lamotte translates it, 'understanding the Law according to the Law.'

'Determining the Dharma according to the Dharma' implies *not* determining the Dharma in terms of that which is not the Dharma. For us in the West this means not trying to understand the Dharma – whether consciously, unconsciously, or semi-consciously – in accordance with Christian beliefs, or modern secularist, humanist, rationalist, or scientific modes of thought, or 'new age' philosophies. The Dharma is to be determined and understood in accordance with the Dharma. To determine it or understand it in accordance with anything else is to falsify it, distort it, and betray it.

In the same way, Dharma worship consists of *applying* the Dharma according to the Dharma. If you try to break off a bit of the Dharma, to take some Buddhist teaching and apply it according to, say, Christian ideas, it just won't work – that is, it won't work as the Dharma. There is no such thing as 'Christian Zen', for example. The Dharma is to be applied according to the Dharma.

Nowadays we hear a great deal of talk about the spiritual life: about 'growth', about 'personal development', even about meditation. But these terms are often used rather vaguely and superficially; few people have a clear idea of what they really mean. And if you don't know what such terms mean, you lay yourself open to what can only be called exploitation. If someone comes along – from the East or, even more likely, from California – and they set up their spiritual shop, advertising this or that technique of personal development, this or that brand of meditation, or even some quite bizarre teaching, and charging quite a lot of money, it seems there is no way of knowing clearly what you would be letting yourself in for if you got involved with them. Without clear criteria to apply, you may get involved with a reasonably positive group or you may get psychologically damaged by a cynical racket – but you won't be able to make *real* spiritual progress. If you have no criteria to apply, you have no way of telling.

So we need criteria for the spiritual life – and such criteria we find in the four great reliances which Bhaiṣajyarāja cites in the *Vimalakīrti-nirdeśa*. The word 'reliance' here translates the Sanskrit term *pratisāraṇa*. *Sāraṇa* means 'refuge', and *prati* is a preposition meaning in this context something like 'about' or 'connected with'. When you rely on something or someone, you entrust yourself to it or to them; you take refuge in it or in them. *Pratisāraṇa* is probably a little stronger in meaning than our word 'reliance', so it is appropriate to call them the 'four *great* reliances' – and this also serves to emphasize their intrinsic importance.

Thurman translates the reliances in the following way: (1) relying on the meaning and not the literal expression; (2) relying on gnosis and not on consciousness; (3) relying on the ultimate teachings definitive in meaning and not insisting on the superficial teachings interpretable in meaning; (4) relying on reality and not insisting on opinions derived from personal authorities.

These four great reliances are not unique to this text, but are to be encountered in many others. For some reason or other, in the *Vimalakīrti-nirdeśa* they are not enumerated in the usual order, but we will look at them in the order in which they are usually presented because this makes them rather more intelligible. I will also change the translation somewhat – Thurman's translation paraphrases a little[68] – and I will put the reliances in the more usual preceptive or admonitory form. Thus we get:

(1) One should rely on the Dharma, not on any person.
(2) One should rely on the meaning, not the expression.
(3) One should rely on the discourses of explicit meaning, not on the discourses of implicit meaning.
(4) One should rely on transcendental awareness, not on discriminative consciousness.

(1) One Should Rely on the Dharma, Not on any Person

The word for 'person' used in this first reliance is *pudgala*, which could also be rendered 'individual'. *Dharma*, of course, means 'the Teaching of the Buddha'. So, 'one should rely on the Teaching of the Buddha, not on any individual'. At first sight, this is rather a strong statement. Does it mean that one should not rely upon one's teachers or spiritual friends? Is it advocating that we should simply read books about Buddhism without having any contact with Buddhists – as some people in fact do?

Certainly not. What this reliance is really getting at is that one should rely on someone only to the extent that they embody the Dharma – not represent it or symbolize it, but *embody* it. The Dharma does not exist in the abstract. There is no such thing as friendliness; there are only friendly people. There is no such thing as joy; there are only joyful people. There is no such thing as meditation; there are only people who meditate. There is no such thing as wisdom; there are only people who are wise. We could even say that there is no such thing as Enlightenment, but only people who are Enlightened. An abstract Dharma is a non-existent Dharma. The Dharma does not really exist in the sūtras. It does not really exist in books. It exists only to the extent that it is practised and realized in the lives of individual human beings.

So relying on the Dharma, not on any person, does not mean abandoning the living Dharma, the Dharma as actually realized by individuals, for the sake of the dead Dharma, the words of the Dharma as preserved in books. We are not being advised to give up on the spiritual community and shut ourselves up in the library, or be self-sufficient in an individualistic way. Still less should we take this as a directive to rely on our own limited subjective understanding of the words of the scriptures. What it does mean, in a word, is that we should not rely on authority.

But what is authority? First, a distinction needs to be drawn between natural authority and artificial authority. An appreciation of spiritual hierarchy, a reverence for those more developed than oneself, is crucial to a healthy spiritual life, and this we could call a response to natural authority. It is artificial authority, spiritual triumphalism, upon which we should never rely. Let's return to the example of the mystic guru. Suppose some new spiritual teacher is expected in town – perhaps from the East, from mystic Tibet, exotic Japan, or maybe from mysterious India – or, indeed, from California. Before he or she arrives, posters and leaflets are plastered all over town. You hear, usually from some devotee speaking with bated breath, that this is a very great teacher indeed, a very great guru – in fact, the rumour is that he is Enlightened. Depending on the tradition to which he belongs, you may be told that he is an incarnation of God, *the* incarnation of God, or just plain God – or you may be told that he is the umpteenth reincarnation of some great spiritual personality of the past, or the head of a huge organization with thousands, even millions of followers who are in possession of all sorts of wonderful, esoteric spiritual secrets.

Eventually the great guru arrives, and a big meeting is organized to receive him. You don't get anywhere near him, of course, although you may catch a glimpse of him from a distance. Then you see him sitting up at the front of the hall, on a throne or surrounded by a halo of electric light bulbs. Next, you hear what he has to say. It is pretty platitudinous, but you are terribly impressed. You believe every word, accept every word, hang upon every word – after all, you have been told that this is an Enlightened master – or even God – speaking. After a few days, he flies on to the next capital city and another big reception. And in his wake a local group is started, advertising his particular technique of 'personal development' or meditation, and you enrol yourself as a disciple – all on the strength of an illusion.

This is perhaps rather an exaggerated story – but it is not exaggerated very much. Such things have happened, and they will keep on happening as long as people continue to rely on a person, not on the Dharma. This is not at all to suggest that there are no genuine spiritual teachers coming to the West – and those who come should be given proper respect. But real spiritual teachers do not make claims about themselves, and they do not allow claims to be made on their behalf. They are not out to impress; they are not after power. Anybody who does make such extravagant claims is not a spiritual teacher but a politician. This needs to be stated strongly because in some quarters there are signs that the great Eastern spiritual traditions are being turned into nothing less than a racket, signs that people are being exploited because they are insecure, because they want to be told what to do by some authority figure.

This first reliance comes, therefore, as a timely warning. One should rely not on claims, not on authority, not on power, but on the Dharma – the Dharma as actually embodied in the lives of spiritual friends with whom one is in real contact and communication. It is spiritual friendship that helps us practise the Dharma, not glamorous but distant spiritual superstars.

This emphasis on contact with the living Dharma, with people who are practising Buddhism, does not mean that we can forget all about the study of the Dharma as presented in the scriptures. The scriptures are the record of the spiritual experiences, insights, discoveries, and realizations of the Buddha and his disciples down the ages, and studying them is a tremendously valuable source of inspiration. But the scriptures are best studied with the help and companionship of spiritual friends. By virtue of their own spiritual experience they will be able to bring the words of the scriptures to life. They will, as Bhaiṣajyarāja puts it, 'determine the Dharma according to the Dharma'; that is, they will explain the Dharma according to the Dharma, not according to preconceived ideas that have nothing to do with the Dharma, or according to their own subjective emotional states.

(2) One Should Rely on the Meaning, Not on the Expression

The second of the four great reliances is advising us to rely on the meaning, not on the expression. In other words, whether we are considering the scriptures themselves or what our spiritual friends have to say about the scriptures, we need to make sure that we are being sensitive to the spirit – not just the letter – of what is being said.

The word translated as 'meaning' is *artha,* but the word rendered as 'expression', *vyañjana,* is rather more difficult to explain. In this context it means something like 'a manifestation or expression of meaning in words'. Such an expression can never be more than approximate; in fact, it demonstrates that words have their limitations – even though within those limitations they can usually do far more than we think they can. We don't find Shakespeare, for instance, complaining about the limitations of language, even though he had more to express than most people. None the less, we cannot understand what someone is saying – or even what the Buddha is saying – if we pay more attention to the way they are talking than to what they are trying to say.

This often crops up in the course of ordinary communication. You may be trying to tell somebody something, but you find, at first to your surprise, and eventually to your annoyance, that they keep picking you up on phrases, figures of speech, even individual words, in a quite unreasonable way. In the end it dawns on you that they are trying to trip you up with words because they don't really want to understand what you are trying to say. They don't really want to communicate, so they are listening to your expression, not your meaning.

Communication is possible only on a basis of openness and receptivity. This means really wanting to understand what the other person is trying to say. The important thing is to pay attention to *them,* to be aware of *them,* because the meaning is after all their meaning. So one should rely on the meaning, not on the expression; on the spirit, not on the letter. This applies to ordinary day-to-day communication, to one's communication with one's spiritual friends, and also to one's study of the scriptures. One should rely on the meaning of the Dharma, not on its expression in words and phrases. Otherwise one is in danger of becoming a mere scholar of Buddhism, someone who may have the letter of the Dharma at their finger-tips, but who does not come within a million miles of its spirit.

(3) One Should Rely on the Discourses of Explicit Meaning, Not on the Discourses of Implicit Meaning

With this third reliance we become just a little technical. 'Discourses' translates the word *sūtras* – that is, discourses delivered by the Buddha, discourses on the Dharma. It is these discourses, of course, which make up the greater part of the Buddhist scriptures. They are very numerous – they are traditionally said to comprise eighty-four thousand *dharma skandhas* or categories of teachings – and they are also very varied, in form, in content, and in other ways. In some cases their meaning is quite obvious; in others, some interpretation is needed.

We can get an idea of this distinction from two simple examples from the *Dhammapada*. Verse 5 of the *Dhammapada* says: 'Enmity does not cease by enmity at any time; it ceases only by non-enmity.' This is sometimes translated: 'Hatred never ceases by hatred; it ceases only by love.' Now, the meaning of this verse is quite clear; it would seem to need no interpretation, because it does not seem open to any misunderstanding. It would not be possible, for instance, to interpret the verse as meaning that enmity does cease by means of enmity. One could not interpret it as meaning that violence or war is justified, or that there could be a 'war to end all wars'. The meaning of the verse is quite unambiguous; it means exactly what it says.

But another verse, from the *Dhammapada* verse 294, says: 'Having killed mother and father, the brahmana goes blameless.' What about this verse? Does it mean what it says? Well, it is clear enough what it seems to mean, but we can hardly leave it at that. It needs interpretation, and this is what, elsewhere, the Buddha himself gives. He says that 'mother' is craving, and 'father' is ignorance; they are called 'mother' and 'father' because they are the root of *saṁsāra*, the root of conditioned existence. To cut this root is to put an end to *saṁsāra*. That is why one who kills 'mother and father' 'goes blameless'.

So here we have the two kinds of discourse: those that do not require any interpretation and those that do: discourses of explicit meaning, as they are called, and discourses of implicit meaning. The Sanskrit is *nitārtha* and *neyyārtha*, or *nitārtha* and *anitārtha*. It is important to be clear about this distinction, and the third great reliance depends upon it. One should rely on the discourses of explicit meaning, not on the discourses of implicit meaning, because the meaning of the former is clear, obvious, and unambiguous, needing no interpretation.

Not only that. Discourses of implicit meaning should be interpreted in accordance with discourses of explicit meaning. The discourses of explicit meaning, in other words, represent or embody the criterion. Your interpretations can be as fanciful and far-fetched as you like. You can bring out all sorts of strange, unexpected and outlandish ideas from sūtras of implicit meaning. This is perfectly legitimate and valid. But what you bring out must not contradict the discourses of explicit meaning.

We can apply this principle to the *Vimalakīrti-nirdeśa* itself. How do the passages in it that deal with all sorts of magical events stand in relation to this third great reliance? There are two points to be made. Firstly, the meaning of these passages is not rational or scientific, but poetic, imaginative, mythic. As such, it makes its own non-rational appeal. The distinction between explicit meaning and implicit meaning applies mainly to discourses of a more discursive nature. But secondly, if these passages are interpreted or translated, so to speak, from the poetic to the rational mode of expression, then the rational expression must not contradict the discourses of explicit meaning.

(4) One Should Rely on Transcendental Awareness, Not on Discriminative Awareness

The Sanskrit words used in this fourth great reliance, *jñāna* and *vijñāna*, are both derived from the root *jñā*, 'to know'. *Jñāna* is pure knowledge, pure awareness, knowledge without any subject or object. It is knowledge which does not know anything and does not belong to anybody. I have therefore rendered it 'transcendental awareness'. It is what Gampopa, describing the *dharmakāya*, calls 'the pure non-dual shine'.

Vijñāna is divided knowledge, divided awareness, knowledge which is divided between subject and object, whether it is between sense organs and sense objects, or between mind and mental objects, or between ego-self and world. It is knowledge which takes place within the subject–object framework and which is therefore limited, or even distorted, by that framework. I have therefore rendered *vijñāna* as 'discriminative consciousness'.

The depth psychology of the Yogācāra enumerates eight *vijñānas*: the five sense-consciousnesses, the mind-consciousness (*mano-vijñāna*), the soiled mind-consciousness (*kliśto-mano-vijñāna*), and the relative store-consciousness (*ālaya-vijñāna*). The work of the spiritual life is to transform these eight *vijñānas*, these eight discriminative consciousnesses, into the five *jñānas*, the five transcendental awarenesses or 'wisdoms' which are symbolized by the five Buddhas of the mandala. There are the Buddhas of the four directions: Amoghasiddhi (the all-accomplishing wisdom), Akṣobhya (the mirror-like wisdom), Ratnasambhava (the wisdom of equality or sameness), and Amitābha (the all-distinguishing wisdom). And the wisdoms of these four Buddhas are all aspects of the wisdom of the *dharmadhātu*, which sees the entire universe as fully pervaded by or as manifesting Reality. This fifth *jñāna* is symbolized by Vairocana, the Buddha of the centre of the mandala. But this is all rather technical. The main point is that the Dharma can be truly, deeply understood only by means of transcendental awareness. It cannot be understood by means of discriminative consciousness. We should therefore rely on transcendental awareness. But that is easier said than done. Before we can rely on transcendental awareness, we must *have* transcendental awareness. And if we don't have it, we must develop it by one means or another.

And one of the means by which a transcendental awareness can be awakened is through the study and exploration of a strange and magical text like the *Vimalakīrti-nirdeśa*. Our explorations here have been, of course, very far from adding up to a complete and systematic exposition of the text. We have looked at only a few of the hundreds of possible themes, taken only a few drops from the ocean. It remains for us to plunge into the ocean itself – the ocean of the *Vimalakīrti-nirdeśa*, the ocean of the inconceivable emancipation.

Notes and References

1 See *Udāna: Verses of Uplift, The Minor Anthologies of the Pali Canon, Part II*, trans. F. L. Woodward, OUP 1948, p.67; also Sangharakshita, *The Taste of Freedom*, Windhorse, Glasgow 1990, pp.16–36.

2 For a detailed exposition of the Spiral Path, see, for example, Sangharakshita, *The Three Jewels*, Windhorse, Glasgow 1991, chapter 13; and Sangharakshita, *A Guide to the Buddhist Path*, Windhorse, Glasgow 1990, pp.93–100.

3 For an enumeration of the eight *vimokṣas*, see *The Holy Teaching of Vimalakīrti, A Mahāyāna Scripture*, trans. Robert A.F. Thurman, Pennsylvania State University Press, University Park and London 1976, p.153.

4 See Sangharakshita, *The Three Jewels*, op.cit., pp.131ff.; also Sangharakshita, *A Survey of Buddhism*, Windhorse, Glasgow 1993 (7th edition), p.480.

5 For a fuller explanation, see Sangharakshita, *Wisdom Beyond Words*, Windhorse, Glasgow 1993, pp.28ff.

6 As in, for example, verse 32a of *The Diamond Sūtra*, in *Buddhist Wisdom Books*, trans. Edward Conze, Allen & Unwin, London 1958, pp.68ff.

7 See Ñāṇamoli, *The Life of the Buddha*, Buddhist Publication Society, Kandy 1984, p.148.

8 For more on this, see Sangharakshita, *Wisdom Beyond Words*, op.cit., pp.262–3.

9 More information on ancient Indian Buddhist cosmology can be found in

Randy Kloetzli, *Buddhist Cosmology*, Motilal Banarsidass, Delhi 1983.

10 For an account of the Mahayana *trikāya* doctrine see, for example, Vessantara, *Meeting the Buddhas*, Windhorse, Glasgow 1993, pp.28ff.

11 For original texts, see the *Larger Sukhāvatī-vyūha, Smaller Sukhāvatī-vyūha*, and the *Amitayur-dhyāna-sūtra* in *Buddhist Mahayana Texts*, ed. E.B. Powell, Dover Publications, New York 1969. For a survey of the Pure Land literature see Sangharakshita, *The Eternal Legacy*, Tharpa, London 1985, chapter 11; and for information on Pure Land thought see Sangharakshita, *A Survey of Buddhism*, op.cit., chapter 3, section 7.

12 See Ñāṇamoli, *The Life of the Buddha*, op.cit., p.39.

13 See W.E. Soothill, *The Lotus of the Wonderful Law*, Oxford 1930, pp.125–128; and Sangharakshita, *The Drama of Cosmic Enlightenment*, Windhorse, Glasgow 1993, chapter 5.

14 See Thurman, op.cit., p.12.

15 Ibid., p.13.

16 Ibid., p.13.

17 Ibid., pp.15–16.

18 Ibid., pp.17–18.

19 Compare this incident with what happens in *The Life and Teachings of Naropa*, trans. H.V. Guenther, OUP 1963, p.105, where Marpa offers all his gold in the form of a mandala to Naropa, but Naropa rejects it: 'Naropa handed the gold back and said: "I do not need it; all that is here is gold," and touching the ground with his big toe turned it all into gold.'

20 Sangharakshita discusses the connection between this chapter and the rest of the *Vimalakīrti-nirdeśa* in *The Eternal Legacy*, op.cit., p.161.

21 The book was Arthur Guirdham's *The Great Heresy*, Neville Spearman, Jersey 1977. It is reviewed by Sangharakshita in *Alternative Traditions*, Windhorse, Glasgow 1986, pp.16–22.

22 From Blake's Prologue to 'For the Sexes: The Gates of Paradise,' in *Complete Writings*, OUP, 1966, p.761.

23 I Corinthians ix.22.

24 Thurman, op.cit., p.20.

25 In some Mahāyāna texts ten perfections are enumerated. In addition to the usual six, the extra four are: skilful means (*upāya-kauśālya*), vow (*praṇidhāna*), power (*bala*), and knowledge (*jñāna*). See Sangharakshita, *A Survey of Buddhism*, op.cit., pp.487–489.

26 For the story of Kisā-Gotamī see *Poems of Early Buddhist Nuns (Therīgātha)*, trans. Rhys Davids and Norman, Pali Text Society, Oxford 1989, p.88.

27 Thurman, op.cit., p.150.

28 See Sangharakshita, *Vision and Transformation*, Windhorse, Glasgow 1990,

pp.60ff.

29 Ibid., pp.18ff.

30 See Sangharakshita, *The Drama of Cosmic Enlightenment*, Windhorse, Glasgow 1993, p.43.

31 Thurman, op.cit., p.22.

32 Ibid., pp.22–3.

33 John viii.32.

34 Thurman, op.cit., p.115.

35 Ibid., p.28.

36 Ibid., p.30.

37 Ibid., p.31.

38 Ibid., p.32.

39 Māra is in a sense a 'devil' figure, but unlike the Devil of Christianity, he has no real power. In practical terms it is perhaps most useful to think of him as personifying whatever gets in the way of one's spiritual progress. For a detailed account of the significance of Māra, see Sangharakshita, *The Buddha's Victory*, Windhorse, Glasgow 1991, pp.21–9.

40 Thurman, op.cit., p.37.

41 Ñāṇamoli, *The Life of the Buddha*, op.cit., p.256.

42 Thurman, op.cit., p.42.

43 Ibid., p.43.

44 Ibid.

45 Ibid., p.48.

46 Ibid., p.55.

47 'Never did eye see sun unless it had first become sunlike, and never can the Soul have vision of the First Beauty unless itself be beautiful.' Plotinus, *The Enneads*, trans. Stephen MacKenna, Penguin 1991, I.vi.9, p.55.

48 Thurman, op.cit., p.50.

49 Ibid., p.66.

50 Ibid., p.67.

51 Ibid., p.73.

52 *The Teaching of Vimalakīrti (L'Enseignement de Vimalakīrti)* trans. Etienne Lamotte, rendered into English by Sara Boin, Pali Text Society, London 1976, p.190.

53 Thurman, op.cit., p.73.

54 Lamotte, op.cit., p.190.

55 On the Yogācāra generally, see Sangharakshita, *A Survey of Buddhism*, chapters 3.8 and 3.9, and Andrew Skilton, *A Concise History of Buddhism*, Windhorse, Birmingham 1994, chapter 15. On the eight kinds of discriminating consciousness, see Sangharakshita, *The Meaning of Conversion in Buddhism*,

Windhorse, Glasgow 1994, pp.66–72.

56 Thurman, op.cit., p.74.

57 The Stream-Entrant is someone who has developed a degree of Insight sufficient to attain to the first stage of the transcendental path, thereby breaking the first three of the ten fetters, i.e. fixed self-view, doubt or lack of commitment, and dependence on mere morality and religious observances as ends in themselves. Traditionally, once one has gained Stream-Entry, progress towards the goal of full Enlightenment is irreversible.

58 Thurman, op.cit., p.75.

59 Ibid., p.77.

60 Ibid.

61 Ibid., p.78.

62 Ibid., p.81.

63 Ibid., p.82.

64 Ibid., p.86.

65 For more information on stūpas see *Mitrata* 74, 'The Tantric Symbolism of the Stupa', Windhorse, Glasgow 1989; *The Drama of Cosmic Enlightenment*, chapter 6, Windhorse, Glasgow 1993; Lama Anagarika Govinda, *Psycho-cosmic Symbolism of the Buddhist Stupa*, Dharma, Emeryville California 1976.

66 Thurman, op.cit., p.91–2.

67 Ibid., pp.98–9.

68 See Thurman, op.cit., p.150, for his remarks on the four reliances.

69 For more of a 'technical' nature, see for example Sangharakshita, *A Guide to the Buddhist Path*, op.cit., pp.51ff. and 61ff.; Sangharakshita, *The Meaning of Conversion in Buddhism*, Windhorse, Glasgow 1994, chapter 4.

Bibliography

The Teaching of Vimalakīrti (Vimalakirtinirdesa) from the French translation with Introduction and Notes (*L'Enseignement de Vimalakīrti*) by Etienne Lamotte, rendered into English by Sara Boin. Published by the Pali Text Society, London 1976.

The Vimalakīrti Nirdeśa Sūtra, translated by Charles Luk, Shambhala, Berkeley California 1972.

The Holy Teaching of Vimalakīrti, A Mahāyāna Scripture, translated by Robert A. F. Thurman, Pennsylvania State University Press, University Park and London 1976.

Sangharakshita, *The Eternal Legacy: An Introduction to the Canonical Literature of Buddhism*. Tharpa, London 1985.

INDEX

BOOKS OF RELATED INTEREST FROM NAB

THE FIRST AND BEST BUDDHIST TEACHINGS

Sutta Nipata Selections and Inspired Essays

—*Susunaga Weeraperuma*

Susunaga Weeraperuma's faithful and masterly rendering of the Sutta Nipata—the oldest sacred book in the Buddhist literature—deepens our understanding of the teachings. An eminent writer in the field of Buddhism, he has lucidly expressed the ancient wisdom using a contemporary idiom. Great philosophical and psychological insights abound this collection of essays. Additional essays address various issues of deep concern and offer practical solutions—on depression, facing death, growing old, finding happiness or world peace.

ISBN: 81-7822-257-4

NIRVANA: THE HIGHEST HAPPINESS

Meditations on Buddhist Issues

—*Susunaga Weeraperuma*

This well-researched and clear-sighted collection of refreshingly original essays offers an enquiry into the Self from the Buddhist Perspective. Though written from the standpoint of Theravada, the author occasionally expresses views that lie outside the mainstream of current Theravada.

ISBN: 81-7822-266-3

THE HEALING POWER OF COMPASSION

The Essence of Buddhist Acts

—*Pamela Bloom*

This book is a collection of remarkable true tables. These tables have the power to transform harmful experience into blessings. Each story is inspiring and illustrates how to heal the heart with peace and joy. Its a must read for all the people seeking the healing experience of Universal Oneness.

ISBN: 81-7822-227-2

THE BODHISATTVA VOW

The Essential Practices of Mahayana Buddhism

—*Geshe Kelsang Gyatso*

The Book explains how to take and keep the Bodhisattva vows and gives clear and practical advice on every aspect of a Bodhisattva's moral discipline, as well as explaining a special practice for purifying our mind and accomplishing full enlightenment.

ISBN: 81-7822-067-9

KALACHAKRA MEDITATIONS

Based On The Discussion Between J. Krishnamurti and David Bohm in The Ending of Time

—***Ramesh Grover***

This book based upon an actual meditative processing of the author's memory recalls, and will be of use to others in keeping a watch, attending to what their mind preceives and reaching out to an understanding of the mischief of thought in perpetuating the delussion of 'I'. The author touches intimately the constricting and suffocating reality of conflict and confusion in one's daily life. The author shares not only his joys and sorrows, as he moves within the movement of the time and thought but also his feel of freedom in the 'ending of psychological time. There is thus a perception of the truth of freedom.

ISBN: 81-7822-279-5

THE ILLUSTRATED ENCYCLOPEDIA OF BUDDHIST WISDOM

A Complete Introduction to the Principles and Practices of Buddhism

—*Gill Farrer-Halls*

The Illustrated Encyclopedia of Buddhist Wisdom is an elegant, straightforward and helpful encyclopedia of Buddhist wisdom. It offers an overview of this ancient spiritual tradition and narrates the life story of Prince Siddhartha; beliefs and philosophies of Buddhism, inspiring quotations from famous teachers and how to meditate in the Theravada, Zen and Tibetan tradition. It wonderfully illustrates the rich world of the timeless wisdom culture, including all the extant schools, practices, teachers and traditions of the Buddhist world.

ISBN: 81-7822-118-7